Regent's Stud

General Editor: F

The Gospel According to John

Responsibility cannot be preached,
only borne.

Václav Havel

Letters to Olga 1983

This book is dedicated to

BARČA VESELÁ

who, in her own quiet way, in her own place, bears it.

REGENT'S STUDY GUIDES

The Gospel According to John

LARRY KREITZER

REGENT'S PARK COLLEGE
OXFORD

1990

Published by Regent's Park College,
Oxford OX1 2LB

Copyright © 1990 Larry J. Kreitzer and Regent's Park College

ISBN 0 9518104 0 5

Printed and bound in Great Britain
at the Flair Press, Northampton

Preface

Like other volumes which are to follow in this series, this book is primarily designed for men and women who are engaged in Christian pastoral ministry, either as ministers of churches or as lay leaders in a congregation. It is hoped, however, that the books will also be of help to other church members who are willing to invest time and serious thought in reading them.

As the title indicates, this is a Study Guide and is not intended in any way to replace larger studies and commentaries on the Gospel of John. I have in mind that it might not only help the reader to consider the major theological issues arising from the Gospel, but might also stimulate some fresh thinking about how the Gospel of John might be studied in house groups and mid-week meetings, how it might become the subject of a stimulating and challenging sermon series, and how it might be used by the individual for his or her own personal devotion.

The chapters of the Study Guide might be divided into four sections of rather unequal length. The first section is contained in chapters 1–3, which are primarily concerned with helping us grasp something of the nature of the Gospel of John as a literary document, seeing how the theology and the writing style of the author mesh together, and to what end. The second section is found in chapter 4. This chapter is designed specifically for the pastor or congregational leader himself or herself. As a study of the Gospel's portrayal of John the Baptist it is aimed at challenging the reader about the nature of a sacrificial approach to ministry.

The third section is found in chapters 5–9. These chapters are concerned with the key theological themes of the Gospel. Each chapter attempts to tackle one major theme with a view to providing enough material to allow that theme to come alive as a focus of a bible study, meditation or sermon.

The fourth section is contained in chapter 10. This is an annotated guide to some of the available commentaries on the Gospel of John. Far and away, this is the thing most requested by pastors, particularly those who have the responsibility of preaching to a congregation on a regular basis. Many want help and guidance on buying commentaries to aid them in their ministry and I have tried in a small way to answer this request here.

I have tried to keep the footnotes in each chapter to a minimum so that the book's readability is not disrupted too much. Where I have referred to other works in the notes I have tried to quote books which are fairly recent and, hopefully, are readily available to the reader. At the conclusion of each of the study chapters (1–9) I have included a few questions and thoughts for further discussion. Some may find that the small-group setting of a church house group might be a good place to explore some of these questions. Others may find that they can be used as discussion starters at local ministers' meetings. Still others may find that they lead to a more personal quest and wish to use them individually.

I would make two final suggestions. First, before proceeding with the study guide, set aside an hour or so and read through the Gospel of John without interruption. Once you have done that write down your immediate impressions and thoughts. Then, as you work your way through the study guide, you may wish to refer to your particular observations, comparing them with those made within the book. Second, when you finish the book, write to me and let me know what you think. In this way a study of John becomes an exercise in mutual exploration for us.

Regent's Park College, Oxford, Trinity Term 1990.   *Larry Kreitzer*

Contents

Preface

1. THE DISTINCTIVENESS OF JOHN'S PORTRAIT OF CHRIST
    1. John and the Synoptic Gospels: a question of harmony
    2. John as the 'Spiritual' Gospel
    3. John as a 'Book of Signs'
    4. The manifestation of glory

2. SOME 'SUTURE-LINES' AND 'FINGERPRINTS'
    1. The continuity of chapters 5–6
    2. The timing of the cleansing of the temple in Jesus's ministry
    3. The crucifixion of the Lamb of God
    4. The literary nature of the Gospel

3. FINISHING TOUCHES: PROLOGUE AND EPILOGUE
    1. The Prologue: a transformed hymn of Wisdom
    2. The Epilogue: final instructions to the disciples

4. RESOLUTION OF A RIVALRY
    1. John the Baptist as Elijah re-born
    2. A Baptist sectarian group?
    3. Some lessons about exercising Christian ministry
    4. A meditative poem on John the Baptist

5. ETERNAL LIFE
    1. The proclamation of the Kingdom of God
    2. Transposition into another key
    3. 'The Hour' of God's possibilities made real
    4. Lifting up to glory: John 12:30–33
    5. 'It is finished!'

6. THE PARACLETE
    1. The Paraclete sayings
    2. Jesus and the Paraclete
    3. The Johannine Pentecost: John 20:22

7. SACRAMENTALISM IN THE GOSPEL
    1. Baptism in John
    2. The Lord's Supper in John
    3. The Sacraments: magical acts or empty symbols?
    4. First communion in Space.

8. THE 'I AM' SAYINGS
    1. 'Egō Eimi' sayings
    2. The Great 'I Am' of John 8:58
    3. The idea of pre-existence in John

9. THE JOHANNINE 'HIMALAYAS'
    1. Johannine christology in light of the Church creeds
    2. The Son of God as 'the Sent One'
    3. Models of christological change
    4. The subordination of the Son

10. AN ANNOTATED BIBLIOGRAPHY ON COMMENTARIES

I

The Distinctiveness of John's Portrait of Christ

It has long been recognised that the Gospel of John is markedly different from the other three Gospels in its presentation of the basic historical facts of Jesus's life and ministry. Many of the best known episodes of Jesus's life are simply not recorded in John. We will search in vain in John for some of the most famous stories of Jesus, many of which are so deeply ingrained in us that they have become constituent elements of our mental picture of the Lord's earthly activities. This mental picture is fostered via the film-image of Jesus Christ which is now a fixed part of our Western cultural religious heritage and which sometimes makes it difficult to appreciate the distinctiveness of the individual compositions provided by the Gospel writers. We are so conditioned by the portrait of, say Franco Zeffirelli's film *Jesus of Nazareth* (1977)[1], that we are virtually unaware of how un-Biblical (in one sense) a production such a film really is. Yet even the briefest of comparisons between John and the Synoptic Gospels (Matthew, Mark and Luke) reveals some sharp contrasts.

For instance, there is no Johannine account of the Sermon on the Mount (as found in Matthew 5–7), or of the Discourse about the End–time (as found in Mark 13), or of Jesus's birth and infancy (as found in Luke 1–2 and Matthew 1–2). Indeed, John's accounts of miracles are rather few in comparison to, say, Mark, where the impression the reader gets is of Jesus the healer on the move, encountering one wounded or damaged personality after the other in rapid succession. For instance, John never recounts an exorcism being performed by Jesus, whereas several are related in Mark. Similarly, the characteristic teaching method of Jesus in the Synoptics, his use of parables, is virtually non-existent in John, with the parable of the sheep in 10:1–18 and the parable of the vine in 15:1–11 being the only serious exceptions. Instead of the heavy emphasis on parables as one of the main methods of Jesus's teaching, so clearly related in the Synoptic Gospels, we find in John a greater emphasis on the personal contact he has with certain key figures. Thus, we find extended accounts about his conversation with Nicodemus[2] in chapter 3, with the Samaritan woman in chapter 4, with the man born blind in chapter 9, with Mary and Martha at the raising of Lazarus in chapter 11. There is nothing quite like these stories related in the Synoptics. Extended discourses are central to John's portrait of Jesus, with the long discourse to the disciples in chapters 13–17 being another classic example.

Perhaps most surprising of all is the fact that Jesus's central preaching theme in the Synoptic Gospels, his proclamation about the coming of the 'kingdom of God', is severely curtailed in John (the phrase 'kingdom of God' occurs only in 3:3 and

3:5, which has an interesting parallel in Matthew 18:3). In its place John has interjected his motif of 'eternal life'.

Relationships between John and the Synoptics with regard to the basic chronological features of Jesus's ministry are another key area of study. Indeed, it often comes as some surprise to discover that the main reason we traditionally describe Jesus's ministry as lasting for three years is because people have taken in a rather wooden way the reference by John to three Passover celebrations in 2:13; 6:4; 11:55 (together with the three journeys to Jerusalem implied in 2:13; 5:1; 10:22 and, possibly, 7:2). But what if, for the sake of argument, these three 'Passover' references, and the associated journeys to Jerusalem, were not intended to be taken as three successive years at all? What if they were parallel descriptions of events connected with a single Passover celebration? What if they were intended by John to be three windows of perception into the same single, highly significant Passover celebration which comes in Passion week? This is not so strange as it might appear to be at first glance. After all, if we read the Synoptic Gospels' accounts carefully, we have no real reason for believing that Jesus's public ministry lasted much longer than a single year. In Matthew, Mark and Luke there is but a single Passover described, the one so closely associated with events surrounding Jesus's own death. Such an interpretation of John would certainly require a revision to the popular understanding of Gospel chronology. But more to the point, how markedly would such an approach to the 'Passovers' in John change our perception about the very nature of the ministry of Jesus? We cannot answer this very complicated question here, but it does serve to illustrate the abiding power of the Gospel of John in shaping our understanding of the foundational issues involving Jesus and his mission.

Lastly, John's distinctiveness as a Gospel is made all the more evident through the inclusion by the author of exalted christological claims about Jesus of Nazareth, claims which seem to go way beyond anything that we find expressed in the Synoptic Gospels. For instance, the addition of a Logos christology in 1:1-4 far exceeds anything that is found in the Synoptic Gospels, including their birth accounts. The idea of the pre-existence of the Word is brought forward to help explain something of the significance of Jesus Christ. While there certainly were some ideas of the pre-existence of divine attributes within the world of Judaism in the first-century CE, the full and complete identification of the Logos with the son of a carpenter of Nazareth named Jesus stands as an incredibly daring theological step for the author to take.[3] Such a complete and absolute 'embodiment' of the Logos into a flesh-and-blood human being means that a new era is entered, one in which the identification of the Logos with Jesus, and with the human situation, is intractable, indissoluble and incapable of being repealed. In short, John makes a sweeping theological declaration which has no parallel within the Synoptic Gospels.

Another example here is the presentation of the omniscience of Jesus within his ministry, again something which is only hinted at occasionally within the Synoptic Gospels. Yet Jesus is presented in John's Gospel as totally in control and unperturbed by the circumstances around him (10:17-18 is a classic example of this). Several passages support this impression of things being determined by God beforehand, including the fact that Jesus seems to know people's reactions to him before they themselves do. Some examples of this can be seen in 1:48; 2:24-5; 4:18-19, 39,50; 5:6; 6:6, 15, 64 and 16:19. The way that Judas is portrayed, almost as if he is merely following orders in fulfilling his role as the betrayer (6:70-1; 12:4; 13:21-30; 18:4), also adds to this sense of divine determinism. Commenting on the Johannine portrait of a Christ who is in control, particularly within the passion narratives, Graham Stanton[4] remarks: 'Jesus remains in control of events: there is no distress or sadness. In the Synoptic Gospels Jesus is on trial; in John it is the captors who are on trial. In John, Jesus is not so much "the man of sorrows", as "the king of glory".'

In short, there are marked differences and contrasts between the way that Jesus's ministry is presented in John and the way it is presented in the Synoptic Gospels. William Temple likened the difference between the Synoptic Gospels and John to the difference between a 'photograph' and a 'portrait' of Jesus.[5] Neither approach, he says, should be at the expense of the other since each serves to illuminate the other. In any event, John's portrait of Jesus is quite distinctive, and his Gospel stands as a highly creative and original written work.

1. JOHN AND THE SYNOPTIC GOSPELS: A QUESTION OF HARMONY

Given this unique character of the Gospel of John, how do we begin to assimilate this fact? How do we explain it? How significant is it? Several things need to be said in response to these questions. First, it is important to stress at the outset that these differences and contrasts are of such magnitude and character that they cannot be explained simply by attempting to construct a harmonization of Jesus's life. This is far too simplistic an answer and means that we actually end up doing damage to the distinctiveness of the actual texts, and destroy the individuality of the various Gospel writers and their message of faith to us, as we attempt to fit them into some logical, reasoned order.

That is not to say that such an approach has been untried, however. Tatian produced the first harmony long ago in his *Diatessaron* (*circa* 150 CE), and there have been adherents to such an approach ever since,[6] but always the exercise is beset with severe problems and limitations. I can still recall one of the most formative experiences in my education at theological college which occurred during my very first term, when I was faced with some of the problems of reconciling the various accounts presented by the Gospel records. My professors kept mentioning things about the differences between the four accounts, and I was determined to settle this matter in my own mind once and for all. I went to a secondhand bookstore and bought several used copies of the RSV text and took them home to my desk. A pair of scissors was found and soon I had cut up the four Gospels into sections, story by story, verse by verse. Having done that I went about trying to put them back together into a harmonized, unified story. The kitchen table was taken over by various piles of papers labelled 'Year One', 'Year Two', 'Year Three' and 'Uncertain' as I attempted to make sense out of it all. I wanted to reconstruct the chronology of Jesus's ministry to my own satisfaction, to make sense historically out of the various Gospel presentations of his life. I tried for several weeks, but eventually found that it was impossible to do so with any degree of certainty. Inevitably, I had to make editorial choices: which story fitted where, and why. At one section I followed Matthew's order, at another John's, at another Luke's (which meant that I had to go against Matthew's), and so on. I soon realized that however I managed to reconstruct the life of Jesus (and believe me, I tried many permutations), in the end there was always a high degree of subjectivity involved. Such subjectivity was completely unavoidable. The experience shook me and challenged my ideas about the basis of the New Testament witness itself. More than anything else it made me realize how easy it is for all of us not to allow the text to speak to us *on its own level*. I had been trying to make it into something it was not (with the best 'evangelical' motives!), and had inadvertently been projecting my own views upon it. I finally gave up in sheer frustration and threw away all of the cut-up sections. Instead, I was forced to accept the text as it stood, with all of its problems and incongruities. I began to discover the supreme joy that comes from not being afraid to allow the texts to stand, with all of their odd angles, unanswered questions, and individual theological signatures. They became living documents for me in a quite unexpected way.

So the harmonizing approach to gospel studies must, in the end, be abandoned if we want to remain true to the text as God has seen fit to preserve it for us. God has, after all, given us four Gospels and not one, as Irenaeus insisted so long ago (in *Against the Heretics* III.11.8). Or to be more precise, we have one gospel in four distinct versions, four highly individualized sketches.

It seems to me that the answer as to why there are such differences and contrasts in the Gospels is to be found at a much deeper, and, paradoxically, a much more human level than is presupposed by such attempts at harmonization. In order to appreciate John's Gospel, we must come to grips with some understanding of not only how the author (whom we shall in the traditional way call John)[7] has portrayed the life of Christ, but *why* he has done it in the way that he has. We dare not forget that however much we emphasize the 'supernatural' dimension in the inspiration of scripture, we are still also dealing here with the product of a human being. He is divinely inspired, to be sure, but that does not divest him of his humanity in producing his work. He does not cease to be a man, but continues to be a flesh-and-blood person writing about his experience of God's grace through Christ. We must try to penetrate into the mind of John himself through what he has written for us. How might we best describe John's Gospel?

2. JOHN AS THE 'SPIRITUAL' GOSPEL

The very nature and character of Jesus's ministry seems altered in John. The 'feel' of the story of Jesus as given in John is different, somehow more intense, more spiritual, more exalted and heavenly, almost as if the song is sung in a higher key. This has long been recognized by the Church and has been acknowledged as the distinctive feature of John's Gospel. Eusebius, writing in the beginning of the 4th century CE, records an interesting comment made by Clement of Alexandria (*circa* 200 CE) concerning the Gospel of John. He notes this assessment by Clement: 'John, last of all, conscious that the outward facts had been set forth in the Gospels, was urged on by his disciples, and, divinely moved by the Spirit, composed a spiritual Gospel.' Perhaps the simplest way to experience this 'shift of theological gears' is to read one of the other Gospels and then follow it immediately by a reading of John. In what ways is it true to say that John's account is a 'spiritual Gospel'? I would like briefly to call attention to several key reasons why John might properly be described as the 'spiritual Gospel'.

First, the fact that John brings together Jesus and God the Father, through his use of 'Son–Father' language, prompts us to this conclusion. Nowhere else in the New Testament do we find Jesus and God spoken of in such intimate terms (we shall have a further opportunity to discuss the centrality of this theme in the Gospel in a later chapter). This familial imagery alerts us to a higher plane of experience, in which Jesus communicates privileged knowledge of God himself.

Second, the fact that there are so many examples of words and phrases carrying a double meaning (having an 'earthly' significance as well as a 'heavenly' one) also leads us to the conclusion that John is doing something more than merely relating the bald facts of Jesus's earthly life. A classic example of this is the way that the word translated 'anew' in the RSV of 3:3 ('born anew') can just as legitimately be translated from the Greek as 'from above', a translation which adds a whole new slant to the meaning of the cryptic passage and actually helps highlight the irony of Nicodemus's misunderstanding. A second example occurs in the same story, this time focusing on the word translated as 'wind' in 3:8a. The Greek term is 'pneuma' which means either 'wind' or 'spirit', heightening the mystery of Jesus's reply in the verse and, in a roundabout fashion, calling attention to the role of God's Holy Spirit in human affairs.

Third, and perhaps most important, the way in which the Gospel itself is put together is partly responsible for this sense of its theological dimension. Luke T. Johnson comments helpfully on this when he says, 'the structure of the Gospel is itself christocentric. That is, it circles about the figure of Jesus. Linear plot development is less important here than in the other Gospels. There is neither suspense nor surprise but only irony.'[8] One of the most important ways in which John displays this christocentrism is through Jesus's continuing to speak to the Johannine church via the Spirit. Again and again we see that the abiding presence of Jesus in the life of the later Johannine community is directly asserted, or suggestively hinted at, by the way John casts some of the sayings of Jesus. We note here, for instance, four key texts, although many others may also be marshalled in support of this point. 10:16: 'I have other sheep, that are not of this fold; I must bring them also, and they will heed my voice. So there shall be one flock, one shepherd.' 16:12–14: 'I have yet many things to say to you but you cannot bear them now. When the Spirit of truth comes, he will guide you into all truth; for he will not speak on his own authority, but whatever he hears he will speak, and he will declare to you the things that

are to come. He will glorify me, for he will take what is mine and declare it to you.'
17:20, 26: 'I do not pray for these [disciples] only, but also for those who believe
in me through their word . . . I made known to them thy name, and I *will* make it
known, that the love with which thou hast loved me may be in them, and I in them.'
20:29: 'Jesus said to him [Thomas], "Have you believed because you have seen me?
Blessed are those who have not seen and yet believe".'

All of this has the desired effect of calling attention to the Gospel of John as a literary
work highlighting the continuing activity of risen Lord Jesus, through the Spirit, in
the life of the Church. What more powerful a description of the Gospel as a 'spiritual
Gospel' could be asked for than this? Moreover, it also has an important contribution
to make to our understanding of the author himself as someone who also serves,
as it were, as an agent of God's Spirit in producing the Gospel. There is no question
of any 'deception' as the evangelist shapes and even adds to the words of the earthly
Jesus; rather, he believes that the exalted Christ is going on speaking through him,
newly, in the Spirit. That surely is something of what Clement of Alexandria meant
when he said that John, 'divinely moved by the Spirit, composed a spiritual Gospel.'
John's Gospel is a 'spiritual Gospel' because it testifies to how the Spirit is *still* working
in and through his people.

A symptom of this approach is the way that the author of John fits together the
short miracle stories and the longer theological discourses, thereby constructing a
deliberately patterned whole (sometimes described as a 'seamless robe'). The result
is that the reader immediately senses the flight towards a higher theological plane
when encountering the thought of John. John soars above the others, ushering us
into a fresh and new understanding of Jesus and his relationship to his divine mission,
leading to his relationship to God himself. Some further comments about this deliberate
structuring of the gospel account are in order.

3. JOHN AS A 'BOOK OF SIGNS'

Do we have any clues as to the reason why the Gospel of John was composed?
Fortunately, within the Gospel of John we have a clear declaration of the author's
purposes in writing, something not expressly found in any of the Synoptic Gospels.
In John 20:30–1 we read: 'Now Jesus did many other signs, which are not written
in this book; but these are written that you may believe that Jesus is the Christ, the
Son of God, and that believing you may have life in his name.' Thus, we see the
evangelistic intention of the writer, his desire that the story of Jesus Christ lead to
faith on the part of the listeners (it is highly probable that this was the original ending
of the Gospel itself and that chapter 21 was added later as an appendix). At the same
time, these verses of 20:30–1 contain one of the most significant terms within the
Gospel of John. It is the term 'sign' (in Greek it is 'sēmeion', plural 'sēmeia'). This
is a highly specialized word within the Gospel, almost bordering on being a technical
term. What does 'sēmeion' mean?

Above all, in John, the term 'sēmeion' is used to signify an event which manifests the glory of God, the presence of God in our midst. In a very real sense, therefore, the meaning of the term 'sēmeion' is much more weighty (in theological terms) than the term 'miracle', at least as it is popularly understood. The point of the 'sēmeion' is not so much about the miraculous event itself, but about the tremendous theological truth to which the 'sēmeion' itself points, the insight into the nature of God that it reveals. This means that the 'sēmeion' is something which is designed to be seen through, something we are to see beyond. It is meant to direct our attention to the truth underlying the 'miracle' itself, to the insight about God brought about by the 'miracle' which is performed. As Barclay Newman and Eugene Nida have commented: 'for the writer of this Gospel there is an inseparable relation between event and interpretation, and so he combines narrative and discourse in a way that may at times seem odd to the modern reader'.[9] It is essential that this be kept in mind whenever we examine the 'signs' (the 'sēmeia') of the Gospel of John.

What of the occurrences of the term 'sēmeion' in John? How frequently is the term employed? In addition to the reference in 20:31 (quoted above), the word 'sēmeion' occurs in John a total of 16 other times, but it is used in a number of remarkably different contexts. In 2:18, 23; 6:2, 26, 30; and 7:31, the term is used in describing the 'miracles' that the people wanted Jesus to perform for them. In 3:2 we find a similar expectation being voiced by Nicodemus. In 4:48 and 6:14 we have Jesus's reaction to such requests for wonder-working when he rebukes them for wanting 'signs'; Jesus recognizes the human tendency to use them as a substitute for true belief and not see beyond them. In 11:47 the Pharisees are said to be worried about Jesus performing too many 'signs', while, ironically, in 12:37 the people are described as unbelieving in spite of the numerous signs Jesus did. This is in contrast to the figure of John the Baptist, who in 10:41 is described as someone who performed no 'sign'.

The final four occurrences of the term 'sēmeion' are in many ways the most important for each is closely associated with a 'miracle' that Jesus performs. Thus, in 2:11 the term 'sēmeion' is used of Jesus's turning the water into wine at Cana, in 4:54 it is used of the healing of the nobleman's son, in 9:16 it is used of the healing of the blind man, and in 12:18 it is used in reference to the raising of Lazarus from the dead. Of these final four occurrences, it is interesting to note the way in which the first two 'signs' that Jesus performs are actually numbered. In 2:11 and 4:54 the miracles are said to be the 'first sign' and 'second sign' respectively.

It has often been noted that there are six such miracles or 'signs' in John (although, as we just mentioned, it is only the first two that are numbered as such). Is this perhaps a clue to the original structure of John's Gospel? This prompts us to wonder whether or not all of the 'signs' at some early stage in the gospel tradition were numbered (like 2:11 and 4:54). This seems a likely possibility. Perhaps they were even numbered by the auther John himself, but more probably such a numbering sequence was contained only within some of his sources and, for some strange reason, was not carried through for the whole of the Gospel. It is impossible to say why this is so.

Rudolf Bultmann, in his classic commentary, suggested that John had at his disposal a 'Book of Signs' source and a 'Book of Sayings' source while composing his Gospel.[10] Recognition of these two basic underlying sources, Bultmann suggests, helps us appreciate the way that John has tended to weave together 'signs' and 'sayings' within his Gospel account into the literary form that we now have. It is extremely difficult to decide now with any certainty what sources John was using, but we can note some of the 'suture lines' of his composition if we examine the Gospel text very carefully. Almost all scholars would agree that the Gospel falls roughly into four major sections: Prologue (chapter 1), the 'Book of Signs' (chapters 2–12), the 'Book of Sayings' (chapters 13–21), and Epilogue (chapter 22).

If, as we suggest is the case, John's primary concern is not a chronological presentation of the life of Jesus, but a theological interpretation of his Lordship for the life of the believer, then can we detect a hint of how John's presentation of this interpretation has helped shape the very structure of this book? This becomes a bit more clear if we list the six 'signs' of the Gospel, the miraculous events themselves, thus:

1. The changing of water into wine at Cana (2:1–12)
2. The healing of the nobleman's son (4:46–54)
3. The healing of the paralytic by the pool of Bethesda (5:1–9)
4. The feeding of the five thousand (6:1–14)
5. The healing of the man born blind (9:1–12)
6. The raising of Lazarus from the dead (11:1–44)

Given the fondness within the Biblical tradition for the number 'seven', the fact that there are only six 'signs' in John may strike us as a little unusual. However, it seems quite probable that this is really a very clever way of highlighting the seventh and most important 'sēmeia' in the Gospel, the resurrection of Jesus Christ himself (as related in chapter 20 of the Gospel). We could go so far as to say that the seventh 'sign' is the empty tomb on that first Easter morning. In other words, each of the previous six 'sēmeia' find their fulfilment in this greatest of all miracles, the Resurrection of Jesus. They all point towards it, each one revealing something about the character of God as one who challenges and changes his people, through his Son, the Incarnate Logos. Each one of the preliminary 'signs' helps to prepare the reader for the most stunning 'sēmeion' of all, the fact that the Son must die and thereby will be revealed as the great conqueror of Death.

Yet, it should not go unnoticed that the six preliminary 'signs' only take us through the first half of the Gospel. It is for this reason that chapters 2–12 have often been described as the 'Book of Signs'. Quite clearly John has supplemented these 'signs' with other blocks of material, namely the Upper Room discourse with the disciples in chapters 13–17 and the Passion story in chapters 18–20. The impression that one is left with is that the number of 'signs' is carefully selected to achieve a specific purpose, to accomplish a particular aim. Once that main aim is accomplished John turns to other things. This means that we should be very wary of assuming John's chronological presentation of the gospel is the point at which we should begin properly to assess his gospel portrait. John's Gospel operates in a much more complicated way than that, revealing to us his specialized version of the good news of Jesus Christ.

Quite clearly, John is being selective in his presentation, deliberately leaving some things open. Or, as he explicitly puts it in 20:30a: 'Now Jesus did many other signs, which are not written in this book'. It is as if John is saying: 'Don't worry about the many other things Jesus did. Concentrate on understanding the meaning of these that I have told you about!'

This leads us to consider in more detail one final motif within John — the place that 'glory' has in his thought.

4. THE MANIFESTATION OF GLORY

Closely related to the purpose of the 'signs' in the Gospel is the idea of the manifestation of God's 'glory'. The term 'doxa' occurs 19 times in the book, almost always in key places (see, 1:14; 2:11; 5:41; 5:44; 7:18; 8:50; 8:54; 9:24; 11:4; 11:40; 12:41; 12:43; 17:5; 17:22; 17:24). It is, for instance, intimately linked to the critical verse with which the hymn of the Logos boldly comes to a climax and stuns the reader with the shocking news of the incarnation. In 1:14 the Logos becoming flesh is immediately followed by the declaration that the incarnation means that 'we beheld his glory, glory as of the only Son from the Father.' This is made all the more meaningful when we appreciate that John has here in 1:14 made a play on words which cannot really be brought out very well in an English translation. The phrase immediately preceding states that the Logos 'became flesh and dwelt among us'. The verb 'to dwell' in Greek is 'skēnoō' and is closely related to the noun 'skēnē' meaning 'a tent' or a 'skin' (which is used to make a tent). The force of the Greek verb is therefore 'to live in a tent' or 'to tabernacle', an obvious harkening back to the Old Testament imagery in which the glory of the Lord comes down to dwell with his people in the 'Tent' or the 'Tabernacle' (as in Exodus 40:34-8). But also, the Greek word actually shares the same basic letters of the Hebrew word 'shekinah' (skn), meaning the 'Glory of God'.

In short, it seems not too far-fetched to say that John is here brilliantly associating the incarnation with the realization of the very 'glory' of God, and that he deliberately exploits the Greek language to convey it. The incarnation of the Logos is John's way of saying that the sign of the 'glory' ('shekinah') has come to 'dwell' ('tabernacle') with us.[11] Thus from the very opening prologue of the Gospel, the reader is alerted to the fact that the message of the story is the manifestation of the 'glory of God' in the person of Jesus Christ, the Incarnate Word. We could even go so far as to define 'glory' as the open manifestation of the presence of God, something which is supremely seen in God's becoming a human being, Jesus of Nazareth. Rudolf Bultmann expressed the close connection between 'glory' and the fleshly incarnation like this: "But this is the paradox which runs through the whole gospel: the 'doxa' ['glory'] is not to be seen *alongside* the 'sarx' ['flesh'], nor *through* the 'sarx' as through a window; it is to be seen *in* the 'sarx' and nowhere else. If a man wishes to see the 'doxa', then it is on the 'sarx' that he must concentrate his attention."[12]

This close association of the 'glory of God' with the foundational declaration of the incarnation of Jesus should cause us to examine our own theology of 'glory'. The 'glory' of God is not some abstract quality about him, an aura that accompanies him, like smoke is associated with fire. Such an association is often suggested by the way that we use the term 'glory' in our hymns and songs. We do have a tendency to speak of God's glory as if it is somehow a quality merely associated with him, rather than its being a descriptive way of speaking about his very presence with us. For instance, we can quite happily sing 'Manifest your glory, Lord' and often what is really going on in our minds is the assumption that God must do something miraculous, perform some unusual event, shock us by doing something completely unexpected, and thereby manifest his glory to us. More often than not the focus in John's Gospel is on the fact that a 'sign' is given to make us realize that God has *already* done something extraordinarily miraculous, that he has *already* involved himself with us and manifested his 'glory' initially in the Incarnate Word, and that he is *already* in the midst of our human situation, continuing to work through the Risen Spirit of that Incarnate Word. It is crucial that we do not set what God *does* and who he *is* at odds with each other in this regard.

How is this related to the 'signs' we have been discussing? The connection is often very explicit and unambiguous in John. He leaves us in no doubt in the matter. For John the purpose of the 'sign' is that it becomes a channel for the revelation of the 'glory' of God, and at the same time it becomes a challenge to faith on the part of those who witness it. This is made clear in 2:11, for instance, where the 'sign' of the changing of water into wine at Cana is linked to the manifestation of God's glory and to belief on the part of the disciples. A similar connection of thought is made in chapter 11 with regard to the 'sign' of the raising of Lazarus. The purpose of this 'sign' is both to manifest God's glory (11:4) and to engender belief (11:40–5).

I suggested above that the seventh 'sign' was the empty tomb of Jesus on the first Easter morning. Strictly speaking, it is incorrect to say that the empty tomb is the decisive *evidence* of Christ's resurrection from the dead. The empty tomb does not 'prove' the resurrection, and was never meant to do so. What it does do is provide an *opportunity* for belief. And this is precisely what we read happens in the case of some of the first visitors to that empty tomb. In John 20:8 we are told that the beloved disciple ran to the tomb that morning and, when he entered into it, began a new experience of belief, to the glory of God, who raised Jesus from the dead. Thus, it is this dual-function of 'signs' — their ability to be both a channel of glory and a challenge to belief — that gets to the heart of John's purposes in presenting the gospel as he has.

This is a very powerful message to us today, because it is alarming how much we have internalized the purposes of 'signs' and 'miracles', making them wholly private affairs which often give more attention to us as recipients than to God and his gracious Presence. Sometimes it seems that we have not progressed much beyond the attitude to miracles exhibited in this child's letter to God:[13]

Dear God,
If you are so smart let's see if you can read my code: VDDL RBT CLJKS NT PSD KLHSM ATFO. If you can read it, make it rain tomorrow so I will know.

                                                                    Gabe

The message of John is that we should never allow ourselves to focus attention simply on the sensational aspect of miracles, whether they be ancient or modern, but recognize the fact that they manifest God's glory and thereby are designed to engender faith. The purpose of miracles is thus always to awaken faith, not only on the part of those who are themselves involved, but faith on the part of those who look on as well. In practice, this means that the 'personalistic' tendency we often confront in our modern world, the tendency to reduce God to a privatized wonder-worker at our own beck and call, needs to be made subject to the larger concerns of life. It is sad how often the relation of what miracle God has performed in our lives is dominated by language of 'I', 'me' and 'mine'. In the face of some of the issues that God calls us to engage with in our world (and thereby manifest *his* presence!), the way in which we concentrate on trivial and inconsequential events ('God helped me find a parking space today! Isn't that a miracle!') can be positively offensive to the non-believer, and ultimately dishonouring to God himself.

In conclusion, John's message concerning 'the glory of God' challenges each of us to consider afresh how we view the miraculous in our world, enlarging our vision of what constitutes 'a miracle of God'. Too often our horizons of what might properly be described as a 'miracle' are very limited, too narrowly conceived and lacking in imagination. We are comfortable with God's activity only within a rather restricted realm; either we adopt a 'business as usual' attitude, or we deceive ourselves into thinking that we want *God's* miracle when in reality what we want is the miracle that *we* expect, or one that suits our purposes, does not inconvenience us too much, and costs us little or nothing.

Yet, God's miraculous action in the world more often than not comes from a completely unexpected quarter, from an oblique angle, through the most unlikely person. It catches us off guard, unprepared, unsuspecting. Think how often it is within the biblical witness, and indeed within the course of subsequent history, that the people of God were unable to anticipate the activities of God within their lives, because the truly 'miraculous' remains far too unpredictable for humans; it is unfathomable, impenetrable. For instance, to turn to an Old Testament example, we can read Isaiah 45 *now* and recognise that the appearance of King Cyrus of Persia on the political scene was truly a miracle of deliverance for the people of God. Yet who would have even dreamed of it *then*? Who would have had the imagination to consider that God would accomplish his saving purposes in this way? I can well imagine that some very traditional and well-respected ideas about God, and how he works in the world, had to be abandoned by many Israelites on that day! A whole new theology had to be constructed after that event! Miracles, true miracles of God, will often fox us totally!

That is not to say that we should not wish and pray for God's hand to work in our world. Certainly not! But it is to say that when a miracle of God does come to us, we may find that can be a very disruptive thing, that it causes us to re-evaluate and reconsider such matters as how we view in issue, and how we perceive our very place within the will of God. In one sense a miracle of God could almost be described as an 'invasion', because it may well demand change of so many other 'comfortable' facets of our life, things we may have worked out long ago. In short, thinking about what is truly 'miraculous' can be a very unsettling thing. And if merely thinking about the miraculous can have such a powerful effect, actually submitting ourselves to whatever miracle of God we discern, becoming swept up in the action of the Almighty, can be positively life-threatening! It may call for us to redefine completely what we consider our own role in helping to bring about his purposes, and that is a very painful, but necessary, step in Christian growth and maturity.

NOTES TO CHAPTER 1

1   It is probably true to say that, through this film, Robert Powell's mesmerizing performance as Jesus stands as the dominant mental image of the Lord Jesus Christ for many people. It is a powerful image, striking us perhaps at a sub-conscious level simply because of the fact that nowhere in the film does the character of Jesus ever blink his eyes. Thus, we are confronted with a Jesus who is wide-eyed and gazing at us relentlessly, penetratingly throughout the whole six hours of the film. This makes a deep psychological impression upon the viewer.

2   Nicodemus is completely unknown within the Synoptic Gospels. Yet in John he is a significant figure, appearing here in chapter 3, in 7:50-1 where he argues for moderation in action against Jesus before the Sanhedrin, and in 19:39 where he comes to the grave with Joseph of Arimathea to anoint the body of Jesus. It has been suggested that Nicodemus was the source of 'inside information' about the trial proceedings.

3   There is ample evidence for a pre-Christian, Jewish belief in the pre-existence of certain divine ideas and attributes, such as Torah, Wisdom, and the Power of God. The Jewish writer Philo of Alexandria (an exact contemporary of Paul the Apostle) has long been an important parallel in this regard, particularly with regard to the concept of the Logos as being pre-existent. John seems to be making a similar declaration about the pre-existence of the Logos, and then taking the extra step of announcing that he has become a human being, Jesus of Nazareth. On this subject, you might like to consult the helpful book by Larry W. Hurtado, *One God, One Lord*, (SCM Press, London, 1988), pp. 41-50.

4   Graham Stanton, *The Gospels and Jesus*, (Oxford University Press, 1989), p. 107.

5   William Temple, *Readings in St. John's Gospel*, (Macmillan, London, 1945), p. xvii. The distinction between 'picture' and 'portrait' cannot be pressed too far, since it is clear that each of the Synoptic Gospels is also a theological 'portrait' in its own right. Having said that, John's is a much more overtly theological portrait, and Temple's suggestion has some validity on this basis.

6   A recent example, by a Baptist, is Orville E. Daniel, *A Harmony of the Four Gospels*, (Baker Book House, Grand Rapids, Michigan, 1987). The text used in this harmony is the NIV, clearly an attempt to accommodate the approach to a modern version of the scriptures.

7   The question of the identity of the author of the Gospel must remain an open-ended one. No one knows for sure who the author was or where he was writing from, or to whom, but traditionally he has been associated with the disciple 'John' who came to live and minister in Ephesus. We do not have to decide the matter in order to appreciate the Gospel we now know

as John. On this question of authorship, see: Stephen S. Smalley, *John: Evangelist and Interpreter*, (Paternoster Press, Exeter, 1978), pp. 47–84. Some recent commentators have argued persuasively for the 'Beloved Disciple' as an 'ideal disciple' of the Johannine community who is projected backwards into the Gospel narratives. For a brief discussion of this, see: Schuyler Brown, *The Origins of Christianity: A Historical Introduction to the New Testament*, (Oxford University Press, 1984), pp. 135–46.

8   *The Writings of the New Testament: An Interpretation*, (SCM Press, London, 1986), p. 478. This is one of the most helpful single-volume introductions to the New Testament currently available. It combines a fluid writing style with a fresh appraisal of the major theological issues at stake in each New Testament document. An excellent bibliography adds immensely to the value of this book.

9   *A Translator's Handbook on the Gospel of John*, (The United Bible Societies, London, 1989), p. 1.

10   Rudolph Bultmann, *The Gospel of John*, transl. G. R. Beasley-Murray (Blackwell, Oxford, 1971). Another extremely influential book which argues for a similar two-source basis for the body of the Gospel is C. H. Dodd's *The Fourth Gospel*, (Cambridge University Press, 1953).

11   The 'tabernacle' image is also taken up in Revelation 21:3 in connection with the vision of the new heaven and the new earth.

12   Bultmann, *The Gospel of John* (see n. 10 above) p. 63.

13   Taken from *Children's Letters to God*, compiled by Eric Marshall and Stuart Hample, (Fount Paperbacks, London, 1977).

QUESTIONS FOR THOUGHT AND DISCUSSION

1. Graham N. Stanton (in his *The Gospels and Jesus* (see n. 4 above) p. 102), has commented: 'It has been said that John's Gospel is like a stream in which children can wade and elephants swim.' In what ways is this an accurate assessment of the book?

2. One of the oldest symbols for John's Gospel is the eagle. Why is this a particularly fitting representation of the book?

3. Use a concordance to look up the following key terms in the Gospel of John: life, light, truth, world. In what ways does John use them as both 'earthly' and 'heavenly' terms?

4. How often do we forgo one or the other of the aspects of 'signs' ('channel' and 'challenge') in our preaching and teaching today? How would such a two-pronged understanding of 'signs' confront the popular understanding of miracles in our world?

5. In 1989 the reforms promoted by Mikhail Gorbachev in the Soviet Union and in Eastern Europe were often referred to as a 'miracle'. Would you consider them to be a 'sign' of God's activity in the world today? Why or why not? In what sense might we describe Gorbachev as a modern-day version of Cyrus (as in Isaiah 45)?

6. If your church has access to a video-recorder, rent or buy a copy of Franco Zeffireli's *Jesus of Nazareth*. Select one or two scenes from the film and show them to your house group as an introduction to a bible study. Ask your group members to read the relevant section from the New Testament and comment about how accurate they feel the film is when compared to the Gospel accounts. Which Gospel version is followed? What additions are made? What deletions are there?

Why do you think that Zeffirelli has done those particular scenes in the way that he has? Keep in mind the following quotation from Zeffirelli about his work: 'Of course, it's obvious that any author or director, whether he is mediocre, modest or a genius, ends up giving a personal point of view just through his very reaction and sensitivity to the material at hand. How he treats it and what he selects, reflects his opinions.'

II

Some 'Suture-Lines' and 'Fingerprints'

Without a doubt the novel *The Trial* by the Czech writer Franz Kafka stands as one of the most creative and imaginative literary works of this century. Although it was only published in 1925, shortly after Kafka's death, it has quickly become a classic work. Its introductory sentence has become a by-word for the modern man facing life within an impersonal society which makes imponderable demands upon him. It begins with these ominous words: 'Someone must have been telling lies about Joseph K., for without having done anything wrong he was arrested one fine morning.'[1] The dark, brooding atmosphere of the novel, in which Joseph K. struggles to discover exactly what is expected of him, and why, by the impersonal authorities which control his life, is haunting. It is so powerful an image that an adjective, 'kafkaesque' has passed into the English language as a description of the literary style, which can perhaps best be described as a nightmare set into writing.

Franz Kafka himself was an insecure man, an alien within his own culture. He was unsure of his own literary abilities, and left strict orders that all of his diaries, novels and short stories be destroyed upon his death. Luckily for us, his friend and colleague, Max Brod, disobeyed this final request and arranged publication of many of Kafka's works shortly after the writer's death in 1924. Posterity would have been immeasurably impoverished had Brod followed the harsh dictates of his friend and burned the manuscripts.

Publication of *The Trial* was not a straightforward matter, however. Brod had Kafka's virtually completed manuscript (of ten chapters), but little idea about the intended order of the constituent parts. In the end he had to arrange them in what he felt to be the best order, setting the chapters in the progression which to him seemed to make the most sense. We can hardly fault Brod for doing the best that he could, but it has meant that ever since there has been serious debate among scholars specializing in Kafka's writing about whether Brod got the chapters in the right order or not. Some Kafka specialists have attempted to re-arrange some of the chapters and thereby make better sense out of the narrative of the book as a whole. In one case in particular, several critical problems associated with the study of *The Trial* are resolved if the order of two chapters is altered. This has led many people to feel that Brod, in the course of editing the manuscript, failed to follow the intended order of the narrative of Kafka's novel. Yet, in spite of the problems about the chapter order the novel retains its powerful attraction and undeniable force. It is still recognised as one of the most brilliant literary works of the century. We could hardly say that its value as a piece of literature is lost because of uncertainty about the original order. What has all this to do with our study of John's Gospel?

The answer is not so very long in coming, since we have some very similar problems of transmission within the Gospel of John. I mention this example from 20th-century literary history to highlight the fact that even the best-intentioned (and well-informed!) scribe, such as Max Brod, sometimes has difficulties in deciding such editorial matters. Brod was a close, personal friend of Kafka and had actually discussed many of the various chapters of *The Trial* with him in considerable detail. And yet, it appears, he got it wrong when he finally was called upon to put the story together. How much more difficult must it be for a document, like the Gospel of John, which has a much more obscure textual history! After all, we really know very little about how the various gospels were put together, and by whom. Occasionally we see some of these inherent editorial difficulties quite readily, perhaps more readily within the Gospel of John than in any of the other Gospels.

Let us examine one or two notable examples which will illustrate something of the complexity encountered when we examine John closely. We begin with a specific problem which shares many similarities to the one described involving Kafka's novel *The Trial*.

1. THE CONTINUITY OF CHAPTERS 5–6

In the first chapter we noted that it is possible to detect some of the 'suture lines' in the composition of John's Gospel. That is to say, sometimes it is possible to see how and why the author of John has put together a story. Like a skilled surgeon he 'sews' together various stories and sections of stories, apparently drawn from a range of sources. Occasionally it may seem to us, however, that the sections are not 'sewn' together very tidily; the 'rough edges' of the document show through. Yet it is extremely difficult to decide if these rather obvious 'suture lines' are in fact the result of the author's own editorial hand as he works through his sources. Another possibility is to say that some of these incongruities arise through the course of the transmission of the text itself through succeeding years, that chapters get shuffled around or pages misplaced along the lines of Kafka's *The Trial*.

Nowhere is this difficulty more apparent than in the curious relationship between chapters 5–6. Johannine scholars have often pointed out that the story of Jesus's journeys is severely disjointed at this point in the Gospel. The basic problem in this instance is one involving continuity of narrative. Let us examine it a little more closely.

We begin by noting that chapter 5 (the healing of the lame man at the pool of Bethesda) is set within Jerusalem. There is no dispute about this particular point; so far so good. But 6:1 abruptly tells us that Jesus went to the *other* side of the sea of Galilee, with no mention being given about how he made the journey from Jerusalem in Judaea back to Galilee in the north. Yet, in 7:1 we are told that Jesus is again walking around Galilee and that he was unwilling to stay in Judaea because of the threat to his life that was present there. The impression in 7:1 is that Jesus is returning from

Judaea to Galilee; but how can this be when the whole of chapter 6, the narrative immediately preceding, is itself actually set in Galilee? Obviously there are some problems in continuity here. How and when does Jesus move from Galilee to Judaea and back again? How might this question be solved?

One simple solution, often put forward by a variety of New Testament scholars from all points on the theological spectrum, is to suggest that chapters 5 and 6 have become transposed in the course of the transmission of the Gospel (similar to what Brod has apparently done in editing Kafka's novel). If we simple rearrange these two chapters into reverse order the problems are solved and the narrative is much more continuous. This means that the movements of Jesus in and around Galilee (as recorded in John 4–7) become much more comprehensible. The resultant order is:

4:47–54 — Jesus is in Galilee
6:1–71 — Jesus goes to the other side of the Sea of Galilee
5:1–47 — Jesus goes up to Jerusalem and ministers there
7:1 — Jesus returns from Judea to Galilee

Yet, this modified arrangement is certainly not without difficulties of its own. For one thing, it does break up some of the continuities of *content* and makes some of the matters discussed within the chapters seem forced and unrelated. A good example is the fact that 6:28–9 does seem to presuppose the discussion contained in chapter 5:39–47. If the order of the chapters is transposed, the logical connection of subject matter appears to be broken. An alternative solution, which seeks to handle some of the difficulties of content, is that proposed by James Moffatt. Moffatt suggests the following order in his translation of the New Testament:

4:47–54 — Jesus is in Galilee
5:1–47 — Jesus is in Jerusalem and ministers there
7:15–24 — Jewish leaders debate over Jesus's teaching
6:1–71 — Jesus goes to the other side of the Sea of Galilee
7:1 — Jesus returns from Judaea to Galilee
7:2–14, 25–44 — Jesus is in Judaea for the Festival

The great strength of Moffatt's re-structuring is the linking together of 5:47 with 7:15 and 7:14 with 25. The teaching material reads much more smoothly, and it has to be admitted that the story seems to flow a little better and make more sense. The point about the continuity of teaching is certainly met, but the geographical movements of Jesus (to and from Judaea, in and out of Galilee) are still in quite a muddle in Moffatt's version. What shall we say about these two approaches to chapters 5–6?

Both of these attempts at re-structuring chapters 5–6 have assumed that the *original* order of the Gospel narrative has somehow become displaced over the course of time. Both have attempted to relieve some of the difficulties that arise from the text by restoring the narrative to the original, intended order of the author. Whether we wish to assign the incongruities of the Gospel of John to the 'untidy suturing' of the author of John, or to a disruption caused by the transmission of the text itself, is a matter which will continue to engage interpreters for many years to come. In any event, the disruption to the flow of narrative in chapters 5–6, in whatever way we feel it may have arisen, should not escape our notice. It is, however, not the only section of the Gospel which has been examined in this way.

There are several other instances when the flow of John's narrative or the consistency of content can be improved by a rearranging of certain paragraphs or short sections of the Gospel (Moffatt's translation of the New Testament is a convenient place to notice some of them). Another classic instance is found in 3:22–30, a brief paragraph which interrupts the flow of the discourse between Jesus and Nicodemus (the conversation carries on much more naturally from 3:21 to 3:31 if we remove 3:22–30 altogether).[2] Another instance is found in connection with the appearance of Jesus before the Jewish leaders, Annas and Caiaphas. Taken as they stand it is very difficult to understand the continuity of Jesus's movements. The order is greatly improved if these verses are rearranged so that they run: 18:13, 24, 14–15, 19–23, 16–18. Another classic example is found in chapters 13–17, Jesus's long, final discourse with his disciples. There are some real problems of continuity within these chapters, particularly with chapter 17, which fits somewhat uneasily where it presently stands. Moffatt attempts to solve this and 'restores' the order of the chapters to 13:1–31a, 15:1–27, 16, 13:31b–38, 14, and 17. Bultmann also recognizes the difficulties of continuity of this unit of text and tries to improve the flow of the text by placing 17:1–5 immediately after 13:30–1, emphasizing the 'glory' theme as a common link between them. We do not have time to consider any further instances here, but most of the major commentaries will provide details.

We are left with something of an open question here. No solution to this problem of the continuity of chapters 5–6 (or to the problem of the order of some of the other passages listed) seems 100 per cent satisfactory. There is no simple answer, but on the whole it seems to me that the transposition of chapters 5–6 is probably the best way forward. This seems so, given the fact that in the manuscript evidence available there are other hints that John has suffered badly in the course of transmission. Perhaps the best example of this is 7:53–8:11, the story of the woman taken in adultery. In many of the oldest and best manuscripts of John, including P66, P75 and Codex Sinaiticus, it is missing altogether. In other manuscripts it is inserted at a variety of places within John, including 7:36, 7:44, 21:25 (and even following Luke 21:38 in one minor manuscript!).

What shall we say in conclusion? In my opinion, the fact that we have this uncertainty about another section of John, namely 7:53–8:11, does seem to tip the balance in favour of those who feel that the easiest way to resolve the narrative problems of chapters 5–6 is simply to transpose the two chapters. On the other hand, it is undoubtedly true that John is such a challenging Gospel that we are always struggling to fathom its meaning, to plumb its depths. This means that what we are picking up as 'geographical inconsistency' or 'lack of continuity' (and trying to solve by rearranging the text) may in fact be *our* problem and not the Gospel of John's.

Let us turn now to a second issue, one which is in some ways even more problematic since it involves what might be described not as a purely textual-critical, or even an editorial matter, but a more complicated theological one. Here we begin to see how John has left his own 'theological fingerprints' on the Gospel.

2. THE TIMING OF THE CLEANSING OF THE TEMPLE IN JESUS'S MINISTRY

John gives us his account of the cleansing of the Jerusalem temple by Jesus in 2:13–25. That is to say, he places it right at the beginning of his account of the public ministry of the Lord. This runs right in the face of the accounts provided by the Synoptic Gospels (Matthew 21:12–13; Mark 11:15–17; Luke 19:45–6), all of which place the event at the beginning of Passion week. How do we account for such a mammoth discrepancy of chronology? Several solutions have been put forward over the years. The first is simply to accept the chronologies implied by both John and the Synoptics and say that there were actually two cleansings of the temple by Jesus; one at the beginning of his ministry (John 2:13–25), and one at the end of his ministry (the Synoptic accounts). This solution is the one adopted by both Calvin and Luther and a number of more recent commentators, including B.F. Westcott, R.V.G. Tasker, and Leon Morris.

On the other hand, a host of other commentators have argued that the 'two cleansings' approach is fundamentally wrong-headed and fails to take into account the essentially theological point that John is making throughout the compilation of his gospel. Included in this group are Rudolf Bultmann, G.H.C. Macgregor, C.K. Barrett, Raymond Brown, Rudolf Schnackenburg, and G.R. Beasley-Murray.

One other theoretical possibility must be mentioned, for the sake of completeness, on this point. It is possible that John's account is chronologically placed at the correct point in Jesus's ministry and that it is misplaced in the Synoptic accounts (one cleansing, but John's Gospel has it right). This is the solution adopted by William Temple, Vincent Taylor and John A.T. Robinson, but it has not received widespread support within the scholarly community. Even so, this suggestion does permit us to acknowledge a larger issue involving what Schuyler Brown has described as a 'scholarly illogicality'.[3] It is certainly true that John's Gospel has at times been neglected as a source of historical information pertaining to the life of Jesus.[4]

Why then does John give us the story of the 'Cleansing of the Temple' at the beginning of the ministry of Jesus? The answer comes in part by closely examining what the cleansing of the temple means in terms of Jesus's ministry. That is to say, that in the Synoptic Gospels the episode is closely related to the decision on the part of the Jewish authorities to have Jesus put to death. In fact, this is explicitly stated in Mark 11:18 (and the parallel in Luke 19:47). John does not include this comment in his relation of the story at all. The closest Johannine parallel to this is, in fact, found in a completely different setting — the raising of Lazarus (11:53). In other words, in John's Gospel it is the 'sign' of Lazarus which sets the wheels in motion and prompts the political machinery which eventually calls for, and obtains, Jesus's death. In Mark (and Luke) it is the episode in the temple which does so.

That is not to say that John's account of the incident in 2:13–25 fails to mention this desire for blood on the part of the Jewish authorities. In fact the cryptic reply in 2:19 by Jesus to the temple authorities presupposes just that. But it is to say that the event of the cross is merely foreshadowed here at the outset of John's Gospel. In moving the cleansing of the temple episode to the beginning of the Gospel, John is in fact free to call attention to the Lazarus incident as the real reason why the Jewish leaders wanted to put Jesus to death. I suspect, that if the truth be told, neither event was universally acclaimed by them as sufficient reason to throw their lot behind Jesus and join his movement. Probably both incidents were volatile and filled with tension. But the emphasis in Mark (and parallels) and John is slightly different on what was the decisive action on the part of Jesus which resulted in his execution.

One final point needs to be highlighted here before we move on. It concerns the quotation from the Old Testament found in 2:17. Here John records Jesus as quoting a rather ambiguous passage from Psalm 69:10 (as in the Septuagint, or Greek version). It is the ambiguity of the final verb 'consume' which is often missed when we read it in English. Most of the time when we read this verse we remember the cleansing of the temple itself and we take the force of the verb to mean that Jesus is just so consumed by zealousness for the Father's house that he cannot bear to see the moneychangers making a profit in the midst of it; and so he is consumed by rage, loses his temper, and throws the whole lot of them out. But the Hebrew word underlying the quotation (which is fairly close to the Septuagint version) is much more dynamic and perhaps gets us a little closer to the truth. The Hebrew verb 'to consume' can also mean 'to consume' in the sense of 'to cause to be put to death'. In other words, it may have the same force as, say, the sentence, 'the fire consumed the house' (the implication being that the house is thereby destroyed and 'dead'). When 2:17 is read in this light the meaning of the verse is shifted away from its being a justification for Jesus's anger to its being a declaration of his impending death. Perhaps this is the real reason why John has chosen to place the cleansing of the temple episode at the begining of his Gospel. It is as if he is saying: 'If you can understand what Jesus says in this story, you will have a good clue as to the meaning of the Gospel as a whole.' The cleansing of the temple thus becomes a prelude for much that is to follow. It is a highly effective way of alerting the reader to the tremendous theological truths that are to come as the story of Jesus of Nazareth is unfolded.

This 'forward-viewing' should not surprise us since it is a technique that we all know from other contexts. We actually encounter it in a variety of familiar ways within our world, in novels and films perhaps more frequently than anywhere else. The best recent example that springs to my mind occurs in Richard Attenborough's film *Gandhi*. At the very beginning of the film we see the fateful events of the assassination of Gandhi in 1948. We watch Gandhi, guided by some faithful servants, move through the crowds of people until he eventually comes face to face with the man who kills him. Then, abruptly, the film takes a completely different tack and we find ourselves back with Mahatma Gandhi at the beginning of his public life in South Africa. The film proceeds through his career in South Africa, his move back to India and his involvement in the events leading to the independence of the nation in 1948. Finally, we find ourselves watching the final scenes of the film and, quite suddenly, we know what is to happen! We have already seen the assassination and here it is before us again, repeated with even greater effect because we know precisely what will happen and we can do nothing about it but witness it again. In the interim we have all but forgotten about having seen the assassination itself already. In this instance the technique of 'forward-viewing' has been used to make a point, and make it very powerfully.

It is perhaps not too far-fetched to suggest that this is precisely what John is attempting to provide for us in the form of the cleansing of the temple incident. The episode thus become a proleptic vision of what is to come within the gospel story. To return to the Gandhi illustration for just a moment, it would be absurd for anyone to suggest on the basis of the film that the Mahatma was in fact assassinated twice (once at the beginning and once at the end). In the same way, it would be ludicrous for someone to stand up in the middle of the film theatre and, as the film approaches its end, shout, 'Now we see that Gandhi is going to be assassinated for the second time!'. To insist on such a literal view of the film's chronology is to miss the dramatic effect intended by the director, to misunderstand his technique. In the same way, it is, in my opinion, stretching the limits of credulity to suggest that John is relating for us the first cleansing of the temple and the Synoptics the second (as is often assumed by many harmonizing attempts). We have to recognize what John is trying to do here and not get hung up on the chronological question alone. There is a more important theological truth at stake and it is that upon which we must focus our attention when we examine the Gospel.

Now let us turn to consider a final passage in which John's theological concerns are also thought to shape how the story of Jesus's life is being told. We turn to the story of Jesus's crucifixion as it is presented in chapter 19. Here we encounter perhaps the most important instance in the Gospel of John where chronological matters are being shaped by theological concerns. Here an even clearer set of 'theological fingerprints' left by the writer of the Gospel of John can be detected.

3. THE CRUCIFIXION OF THE LAMB OF GOD

The critical question here is 'when was Jesus crucified?' It is important to emphasize in our discussion of this question that the fact of the crucifixion is not being disputed, not its theological significance in terms of its being the atoning act of God, merely its precise timing. How does such a problem arise? In order to answer this, we must first have a brief look at the timing of the crucifixion in the Synoptic Gospels.

In Mark 14:12–31 (the parallels are in Matthew 26:17–30 and Luke 22:7–23) we are told that the last supper that Jesus shared with his disciples was also a Passover meal and that it was celebrated on the first day of the Feast of Unleavened Bread. This would be the evening of Thursday/Friday (in the Jewish calendar it is Nisan 15 which ran from 6:00 p.m. to 6:00 p.m. After the meal Jesus goes to the garden at Gethsemane and is arrested and tried during the night. Jesus is crucified on the next day, that is to say, on Friday morning at about 9:00 a.m. (Mark 15:25). He dies approximately six hours later, at about 3:00 in the afternoon (Mark 15:34). Thus far so good. There are no major problems with the chronology of the crucifixion events as they are portrayed in the Synoptics.[5]

When we come to the account in John, however, we encounter a real difficulty for he alters the basic chronology in a significant way. Five verses from John are central to this discussion: 13:1; 18:28; 19:14, 31, 42. Let us examine them each in turn. Firstly, in 13:1 we see that the Feast of the Passover is approaching (how soon is left open). The important point here is that the whole of the rest of the chapter is John's account of Jesus's last supper with the disciples. That is to say, we are left with the clear impression that the last supper was *before* the Passover feast and that it was *not* a Passover celebration (the Greek word 'pro' ('before') in 13:1 is quite explicit).

Second, in 18:28 we encounter another bit of chronological information where it is said that, following Jesus's arrest, the Jewish leaders take him to the Praetorium so as to present him to Pilate. However, the verse goes on to say that they would not enter the Praetorium, because they did not want to defile themselves and thereby be unable to eat the Passover meal. The implication is that this presentation before Pilate takes place the day before the Passover itself (that is to say, early on Thursday morning, which is, according to the Jewish calendar, Nisan 14). This also means that we must place the last supper story as given in chapter 13 as having taken place the previous night (also on Nisan 14, remembering that in Jewish reckoning days run from 6:00 p.m. to 6 p.m.).

Third, we come to the three verses in chapter 19. In verse 14 it is explicitly stated that Jesus was crucified on the day of preparation for the Passover (the timing of the crucifixion on this day is the same as that mentioned in Mark 15:25, 9:00 a.m.). But the critical point is that the Greek gives us a rather technical phrase (paraskeue tou pascha) which is best translated as 'the eve of Passover' or 'the day of preparation for the Passover'. This does not mean the evening of Passover itself (that is to say, on Friday evening), but on the previous evening (Thursday evening). Thus, the phrase 'the eve of Passover' has much the same sense that 'Christmas eve' does in English; 'Christmas eve' does not mean the night of December 25th but the evening before Christmas, that is to say, December 24th. In other words, Jesus is clearly said in John's Gospel to have been crucified on Thursday afternoon (Nisan 14). This is in contrast to the account of Mark (and Matthew and Luke) which states, as we saw a moment ago, that he was crucified on Friday afternoon (Nisan 15).

This Johannine chronology is confirmed by the other two relevant verses from chapter 19. In verse 31 we find that the Jews ask Pilate to allow Jesus's body to be taken down and buried because it was the 'day of preparation for the Passover', or as we could say, 'eve of the Passover'; while in verse 42 we find that the body of Jesus is laid in an empty tomb 'on account of its being the eve of the Passover'. This is simply another way of stating that there was concern to remove the body and place it in the tomb before the Passover began. Presuming that Jesus's death occurred at 3:00 p.m. this means that they were in a hurry to finish the job because the Passover started at 6:00 p.m.

There have been several attempts to explain this discrepancy in John's chronology. Some have suggested that John's Gospel was following a different calendar from that of the Synoptic Gospels, or that a Greek view of the counting of days was being used. But the long and short of it is that all such suggestions often end up creating more complications than they solve. The fact of the matter is that John has shifted the chronology backwards one day and that his timing of the crucifixion events is thereby incompatible with that contained in the Synoptic Gospels. Having said all of that, what does it mean? The important question is: *why* has John done this?

The answer comes, I think, through the simple recognition that it was customary for Jews to slaughter the Passover lambs used in their celebration meals on the Thursday, Nisan 14. Apparently John has creatively rolled the clocks back for one day so that he can associate the death of Jesus with the slaughter of these lambs. We have one other brief clue from the Gospel which supports this as the explanation — John's understanding of Jesus as the 'Lamb of God'. John clearly sees Jesus in terms of his being the Passover lamb, as can be evidenced by the declaration of John the Baptist at Jesus's baptism. In 1:29 the Baptist proclaims: 'Behold the lamb of God who takes away the sins of the world.' Interestingly, this is a declaration not found in the Synoptic accounts. What does it mean?

I would like to suggest that by this declaration on the part of John the Baptist in 1:29 the death of Jesus is being invested with tremendous theological significance. There are some indications that this investment takes place very early within the Christian movement. Paul describes Christ in 1 Corinthians 5:7 as 'our Passover who has been sacrificed' (the letter is dated to about 57 CE). At the same time, we should note that the vision of the Lamb in Revelation 4–5 is filled with sacrificial imagery drawing upon the idea of Christ as the Passover lamb (we can date the Apocalypse to about a decade after John's gospel, *circa* 100 CE).

It seems clear that the idea of a 'Lamb of God' theology takes root very quickly and yields a rich harvest of theological reflection in early Christian writings. At the same time it has become a very important theme in Christian art throughout the centuries. Many significant paintings and musical compositions draw upon it for their inspiration. Take, for instance, the famous Isenheim alterpiece, painted by the German artist Mathis Grünewald in the fifteenth century and now exhibited at the Unterlinden Museum in Colmar, France. The central panel portrays a mottled and broken Christ hanging on the cross, head twisted sideways and resting on his breast. Perhaps the most striking feature of Jesus is his cramped fingers, grotesquely reaching heavenward as a gesture of appeal for divine mercy. Standing alongside the cross is a portrait of John the Baptist, his right index finger pointing suggestively toward the crucified Christ as if to say that this is the one to whom his message was directed. At John's feet is the small, almost forgotten, figure of a white lamb bearing a small cross. The whole scene is one of the most graphic representations of the crucifixion ever produced and remains with the viewer long after it is first seen. Anyone viewing the painting would be left in no doubt about the powerful 'Lamb of God' imagery underlying it. It is without doubt that a 'Lamb of God' theology has been one of the most important legacies of the Johannine presentation of the Christ-event that the Church has. It stands as a supreme theological interpretation of what Jesus's death means.

All of this is to say that the historicity of Jesus's death is not enough. The fact of Jesus's death must be properly filled out with theological meaning, the atoning significance found within it. It is one thing to say that Jesus died nearly two thousand years ago on a Roman cross in Judaea while Pontius Pilate was procurator. It is quite another to say that his death does something for us, that it accomplishes everything for our relationship with God. The first assessment of the cross rests on the level of history; the second rests on the level of theological truth. It is the second of these with which John is primarily concerned and his re-ordering of the chronology of Jesus's crucifixion stands as prime evidence. All of these things will cause us to consider anew the very nature of the Gospel of John as a literary document.

4. THE LITERARY NATURE OF THE GOSPEL

Perhaps the main lesson to be drawn from our discussion here is one concerning the literary nature of the written documents with which we are working. We need to be careful that we do not demand historical precision and scientific logic where it is neither intended by the writer nor appropriate for the kind of writing before us. This is true for all the biblical texts, and it seems particularly important when we come to consider the Gospel of John. C.K. Barrett comments about the stories contained in the Gospel in this way:

> Since the material is disposed in accordance with a theological and literary scheme, it is idle to seek in John a chronology of the ministry of Jesus. This is not to deny the existence of valuable historical material in John; but the material has been digested and expressed organically in an organism which is primarily theological.[6]

This need not frighten us, or make us fear unduly for our faith. Instead it should enliven us to the reality of what a miracle it is that God can still perform his saving work through such documents which are transmitted and preserved through human hands. An illustration might help us grasp what is meant.[7]

Everyone is familiar with the famous logo of the American recording corporation RCA Victor, known in Britain as HMV. We have all seen enough gramophone records and tapes to recognize immediately the evocative image of the dog sitting by the old-style gramophone with his head cocked to one side, listening intently to the sound coming forth from the trumpet. The motto of the RCA company was, of course, 'His Master's Voice' (hence the British abbreviation) and the idea behind the advertisement image was that the records and tapes produced by the company were so true to the original that the dog could recognize his master's voice through listening to them. The illustration is a good one (if not pressed too far!) to apply to our understanding of the biblical texts in that through them we too can hear the Master's voice.

However fine and moving a record may be, we should not confuse the grooves that have been cut with the living voice itself. The record may even, through use over the years, become scratched and warped, so that there may be distracting 'pops' and 'crackles' as it is played. But for all this, the faithful listener will still be able to recognize his master. In the same way, the written texts of scripture cannot be *exactly* the same as that living Word of God who is a person, Jesus Christ; but they are inspired witness to him. They may even have become slightly re-arranged in the course of transmission over the generations. But this does not matter in the end. We can still hear through them the Master's voice, calling us to a saving relationship with Jesus Christ. He should be the focus of our faith.

Indeed, far beyond what is true of any gramophone record, we actually *meet* the Master who is speaking to us in Christ as we read scripture. It is nothing less than a place of *encounter* with the Word of God.

NOTES TO CHAPTER 2

1   The main character in the novel, Joseph K., is a loosely disguised portrait of Kafka himself, who struggled all of his life with his double-damnation of being both a Jew and a German-speaking Czech in the city of Prague, which was predominantly Catholic and Czech-speaking. In the sister novel *The Castle* the main character, again a portrait of Kafka, is depersonalized even further, being known simply as 'K.'.

2   Usually 3:22–30 is then placed between 2:12 and 2:13. This makes sense considering Jesus is then said to go to the land of Judaea (3:22) before his arrival in Jerusalem (2:13).

3   Schuyler Brown, *The Origins of Christianity: A Historical Introduction to the New Testament,* (Oxford University Press, 1984), p. 35.

4   The reassessment of John as an historical source lies at the heart of John A.T. Robinson's *The Priority of John,* (SCM Press, London, 1985), which attempts to argue for a pre-70 CE date for the Gospel. Robinson is here building on ideas expressed in his earlier book *Redating the New Testament,* (SCM Press, London, 1976), pp. 254–311. Although much of what Robinson has to say on this matter is highly speculative and would therefore be subject to considerable scholarly debate, he stands as one of the most creative and original interpreters of John within the English-speaking world in recent years. Also, on this subject of John's historical value, see: Craig Blomberg, *The Historical Reliability of the Gospels,* (IVP, Leicester, 1987), pp. 153–189, who cites some of Robinson's ideas approvingly.

5   Some have argued that there are internal inconsistencies within the Synoptic Gospels themselves, but in my opinion there is no real ground for this. A more interesting possibility is that the Johannine chronology is historically correct and the Synoptic chronology incorrect. The point is that both cannot be historically accurate; one must decide one way or the other.

6   C.K. Barrett, *The Gospel According to St. John,* 2nd edition, (SPCK, London, 1978), p.15.

7   This illustration is drawn from Emil Brunner's *Our Faith,* (SCM Press, London, 1936), p. 19–20.

QUESTIONS FOR THOUGHT AND DISCUSSION

1. In what sense is it correct to say that John has sacrificed chronology for sake of his theology? Compare and contrast some of the major commentaries on this point (a good focal passage for this is John 2:13–25, the 'Cleansing of the Temple' episode).

2. Examine the order of the Gospel of John within Moffatt's translation. Why do you think he suggests the alterations in the order that he does?

3. John Barton, in his *The People of the Book?*, (SPCK, London, 1988), p. 58, states: 'I believe that Christians exist principally in relation not to a text but to a person.' What do you think that he means by this? Is it a helpful way to proceed or not?

4. Pastorally, how would you respond to someone who came to you and said, 'If John could make a mistake when he was writing about something as central as the crucifixion of Jesus, then how can I trust his testimony at all?'

5. Find a reproduction of the Isenheim Altarpiece. Examine it closely for other Johannine motifs. What feelings and thoughts does the painting evoke within you?

III

Finishing Touches: Prologue and Epilogue

Hopefully, by now we have begun to appreciate something of the rich tapestry that is the Gospel of John. We have noted some of its distinctive features in terms of sources, structure, style and theological emphases. These are all important to enable us to appreciate the document as a living, life-breathing text. It is important to understand that it did not simply drop out of the heavens and come to us ready-formed. The Gospel had to undergo the various processes of transmission that all such early Christian documents did, processes which show us, above all, how the early Church came to grasp the meaning of her faith and sought to express this faith in written forms. Thus, the Gospel of John is by no means unique in this regard. It shares the literary heritage of the rest of the New Testament witness.

Nevertheless, the Gospel of John has been subject to a considerable amount of extra scholarly attention in these matters, mostly because of its richness and significance as a theological document. On a practical level this means that one of the most helpful things to keep continually in mind whenever we read a section of John's Gospel is to ask where that individual unit might be placed in the history of the development of the text.[1] Does the passage we are reading seem to reflect early Christian preaching or hymns of worship which the evangelist has taken up and used for his purpose? Does it seem to indicate that earlier material is being used to illuminate later difficulties and confrontations being experienced by a subsequent generation of the Church? Is this causing that traditional material to be reshaped and in what way? Keeping these ideas in mind, Robert Morgan and John Barton have usefully described the Gospels in this way: 'The Gospels are doubly exposed photographs, containing two (or more) pictures superimposed upon one another'.[2]

In short, we must be listening for what is going on behind the words of the text, what lies between the lines, as well as paying attention to the actual words of the text itself. Doing this keeps us attentive to the forces which have helped shape the passage and thereby enables us to understand the text at a much deeper level than might be possible otherwise. This is a very difficult, but essential task for the exegete to perform.

Within this chapter we will concentrate our attention on two passages from the Gospel which are almost universally assigned to the final stage of the development of the book, whenever we feel that might have been. These two passages are the Logos hymn (1:1–18) and the account of the resurrection appearances by Jesus to the disciples (chapter 21). Thus we are focusing on both the Prologue and the Epilogue of the Gospel, passages which might be described as the finishing editorial touches of the document. First we turn to the Prologue in 1:1–18.

1. THE PROLOGUE: A TRANSFORMED HYMN OF WISDOM

It is probably true to say that the Prologue of John 1:1–18 has been the cause of more ink being poured out onto paper than any other single passage in the New Testament. The amount of scholarly investigation into the Prologue of John is staggering and it is virtually impossible for anyone to keep up with all of it. This in itself is a testimony to the importance of the passage within New Testament research, particularly with regard to its contribution to the study of early Christian christological thought. James D.G. Dunn[3] has remarked on the impact that John's Gospel, notably through the Logos Hymn of 1:1–18, has had upon the church: 'In a real sense the history of christological controversy is the history of the church's attempt to come to terms with John's christology — first to accept it and then to understand and re-express it.' John's Prologue of 1:1–18 is seen by many to be the most exalted christological statement within the whole of the New Testament. Certainly it stands alongside the concept of 'Son of God' as the 'twin peaks' of John's message about Christ (we will have more to say about this in the final chapter of the book).

We have already said something in chapter 1 about the meaning of the critical verse of the Prologue, the astonishing declaration of 1:14 that the 'Word became flesh and tabernacled with us.' What an absolutely staggering sentence that is! So awesome a declaration is this that it is difficult, one could go so far as to say, impossible, to fathom the depths of its meaning.

Our aim at this point is a much more restricted one. Here we focus our attention upon another aspect of the Prologue, namely its incorporation of pre-Christian material. It seems clear that John has taken over a rather philosophical poem or hymn about the Logos ('Reason' is perhaps nearer the mark as the original translation of 'Logos' than 'Word' is in this regard). Several attempts have been made at delicately 'dissecting' the pre-Christian hymn away from the surrounding material. The results have not been unanimous, but a fair degree of consensus about the matter has emerged. Most feel that the pre-Christian poem about the Logos included sections of 1:1–5, 9–12, and perhaps verses 14 and 16. As a slight variation to this, I would like to propose the following as a reconstruction of the original hymn:

> (Stanza 1)   In the beginning was the Logos
> and the Logos was with God.
> The Logos was God
> and was in the beginning with God, creator of *all*.

> (Stanza 2)   *All* things came into being through him
> and apart from him not one thing came into being.[4]
> That which came into being, was life in him,
> and the life was the *light* of humankind.

(Stanza 3)   The *light* shines in the darkness,
              and the darkness can not put it out.
              It is the true light
              which shines on everyone coming into the *world*.

(Stanza 4)   The *world* came into being through him,
              and the world did not know him.
              He came into his own,
              and his own did not receive him.
              But as many as did receive him,
              he gave them authority to become children of God.

The strength of a proposal such as this is that it divides the hymn into four stanzas which have as their focus key theological concepts, most which are developed and explored further throughout the rest of the Gospel. Thus, the four stanzas concentrate on Logos, life, light, world/children, respectively. As we have reconstructed the hymn, the final line of each stanza contains the essential idea with which the next stanza begins (as the words in italics demonstrate). This 'inter-locking of ideas' is a technique which was quite common in religious hymns of the ancient world.

Somewhat unexpectedly, the 'Logos' idea is not ever picked up again as a theme in the rest of the Gospel; it never occurs outside of chapter 1. Some have felt that this is the firmest evidence that 1:1–18 is indeed a Prologue to the work as a whole and that it was added at the final stage of editing of the Gospel, after the evangelist responsible for shaping the main contents of the Gospel had done his work. I believe this is probably correct, but is it demanded? When one thinks about it for a moment, it is not necessarily so straightforward. Suppose the evangelist *also* re-shaped the Logos hymn and himself placed it at the beginning of his book. Then how *could* he develop the Logos theme further within the gospel? What could one do for an encore, so to speak? It may well be that the lack of repetition of the theme within the main body of the book is simply a means of drawing attention to the incredible statement in 1:1–14. In other words, by not following through with the theme, attention is thereby directed to this initial assertion about the incarnation of the Logos.

It is important to note that there is nothing distinctively Christian within the original hymn as we have reconstructed it. There is nothing which necessarily marks it out as the product of a Christian writer who is grappling with explaining the revelation of God as it has come most fully in Jesus Christ. In fact, the explicit incarnational declaration linking the Logos to a human being is, as we said, withheld until verse 14. What is the meaning of this particular observation?

The answer to this is that such a (re-constructed) hymn makes perfect sense in a non-Christian, Jewish context. That is to say, that it is exactly the sort of thing that a philosophically-minded Jew, such as Philo of Alexandria, might say about God's wisdom. Such a hymn could easily stand as a poem in praise of the personification of an attribute of God — his Wisdom. In this way the hymn embedded within John 1:1–18 shows a remarkable similarity in terms of content and thought to Proverbs 8, an extended poem on God's wisdom. Or, alternatively, Wisdom of Solomon 7 and Wisdom of Ben Sirach 24 have also been seen by some as important parallels. Note the following passages dealing with wisdom, the first written in the third person and the second in the first person:

Wisdom of Solomon 7:24–27: 'For wisdom is more mobile than any motion; because of her pureness she pervades and penetrates all things. For she is a breath of the power of God, and a pure emanation of the glory of the Almighty; therefore nothing defiled gains entrance into her. For she is a reflection of eternal light, a spotless mirror of the working of God, and an image of his goodness. Though she is but one, she can do all things, and while remaining in herself, she renews all things; in every generation she passes into holy souls and makes them friends of God and prophets.'

Wisdom of Ben Sirach 24:3–9: 'I came forth from the mouth of the Most High, and covered the earth like a mist. I dwell in high places, and my throne was in a pillar of cloud. Alone have I made the circuit of the vault of heaven and have walked in the depths of the abyss. In the waves of the sea, in the whole earth, and in every people and nation I have gotten a possession. Among these I have sought a resting place; I have sought in whose territory I might lodge. Then the Creator of all things gave me a commandment, and the one who created me assigned a place for my tent. And he said 'Make your dwelling in Jacob, and in Israel receive your inheritance.' From eternity, in the beginning, he created me, and for eternity I shall not cease to exist.'

When examined carefully, some of the parallels to John 1:1–18 contained within these two texts are quite striking. The key point is that we best understand the significance of the Logos poem contained in the Prologue of John if we examine it first of all as a Jewish hymn which originally had as its focal point the Wisdom of God. Once we gain an insight into what it meant in terms of its non-Christian setting, then we can better understand how the re-working of the hymn in the Gospel has completely transformed its theological meaning. All of this is a rather roundabout way of highlighting the creativity and ingenuity of the final editor (or of the evangelist himself) in using a contemporary Jewish hymn of praise to God's Wisdom as a vehicle for asserting christological truth about Jesus Christ. For this reason George Beasley-Murray comments: 'The employment of the Logos concept in the prologue to the Fourth Gospel is the supreme example within Christian history of the communication of the gospel in terms understood and appreciated by the nations.'[5]

Perhaps the main practical lesson to be learned from this is the way in which the person who gave final shape to the Gospel of John has turned to contemporary society for material to help him communicate the full wonder of the incarnation as he understood it. Everything becomes a potential channel for his theology and he is quite happy to utilize other people's ideas and concepts if they help him in the end open the windows of understanding to the significance of Jesus Christ. The lesson is a salient one for us to keep in mind within our own situations. There is a real sense in which we are all called to discover fresh, new and creative ways in which the reality of the incarnation can be brought home to the people with whom we serve as ministers or as Christian workers. We now turn to our second consideration.

In chapter 21 we have an account of a post-resurrection appearance of Jesus to his disciples alongside the Sea of Galilee. The first thing that needs to be said about this chapter is that it has all the classic signs of being an appendix. It reads almost as if it were an afterthought, following awkwardly on from the end of the previous chapter. More importantly, the fact that 20:30–1 reads so much like the original conclusion of the Gospel makes any other way of understanding chapter 21 difficult to imagine. In short, we are driven to the conclusion that chapter 21 was probably added after the main body of the Gospel was completed. When this happened is impossible to state with certainty, but it must have happened very early on since no major manuscripts of John stand without it. A date of perhaps 90 CE for the final edited form of the Gospel of John is perhaps not too far amiss.

The geographical setting of chapter 21 has been a prime factor in stimulating study of it. In some ways, the Galilean setting of the story is almost as important as the fact that it relates a resurrection appearance by Jesus. Why is this so? In order to understand this we must briefly look at the resurrection appearances as they are related by the Synoptic Gospel writers. Let us examine the Synoptics in the order Mark, Matthew, Luke.

Firstly, in Mark 16 we are immediately faced with a major textual problem, one which has immense implications for the study of the Gospels as a whole. The ending of Mark's Gospel is by no means certain. Two endings survive in the manuscript evidence available, both of which are given in most good translations. Did the Gospel originally end at verse 8? Or did it end at verse 20? This is the (in)famous problem about the shorter or longer ending of Mark. If Mark 16:8 was the original ending then we are faced with the curious fact that Mark's Gospel, the earliest Gospel, contains no resurrection *appearances* (though the resurrection is *announced* by an angel). This is a problem of no little significance, especially if, as most Christians have always believed, the resurrection of Jesus on the first Easter Sunday stands as the foundation of our faith. The problem is made all the more critical when it is remembered that Codex Sinaiticus, one of the oldest and best uncial manuscripts we have, contains Mark's shorter ending (that is to say, it ends at 16:8). We are thus faced with the awkward fact that our earliest text of Mark's Gospel contains no story of Jesus's resurrection appearances to the women or to the disciples.

Assuming for the moment that Mark's Gospel did originally end at 16:8 (something which is hypothetical and will be discussed more fully below), how does that affect the meaning of the resurrection appearances of Jesus as recorded in Matthew and Luke? Both of those Gospels do contain accounts of Jesus's resurrection appearances to various disciples, but, and this is the critical point, they have somewhat different geographical settings. Matthew 28:1–10 describes Jesus's appearance to Mary and Mary Magdalene outside the tomb (verses 1–7), as well as the appearance to the disciples (verses 8–10). Both of these take place in Jerusalem. Matthew 28:16–20 also contains further appearances to the disciples in *Galilee*.

Luke's account, on the other hand, is somewhat different, with a rather fuller description and additional details. His account of the appearance of Jesus to Mary and Mary Magdalene in 24:1–10 is very similar to that recorded in Matthew and his account of the appearance to the disciples, notably Peter in 24:11–12, is perhaps compatible with Matthew 28:8–10. However, Luke goes on to give details of an extra appearance, namely to the two disciples on the road to Emmaus (24:13–35). This is then followed by another appearance to the disciples in which he challenges them to greater belief and witness (24:36–49). The Gospel of Luke then concludes with a brief paragraph describing Jesus's ascension to heaven and the return of the disciples to the city of Jerusalem (24:50–3). This last point is particularly important for it means that the resurrection appearances of Jesus in Luke are all within a Jerusalem (Judaean) setting. So where does all of this take us so far?

In short, it means that we find questions arising in the minds of some not only about whether Jesus ever did appear to anyone (remembering that Mark does not specifically say so!), but *where* such (alleged?) resurrection appearances took place. If we were to begin with the complete absence of details of resurrection appearances in Mark, and were then to conclude that the resurrection appearances in Matthew and Luke are in a state of hopeless confusion (they cannot even get straight between them where it is that Jesus shows himself!), then we could readily see how scepticism about the truth of the resurrection might be allowed to reign. This has led some scholars, such as Norman Perrin for instance, to attempt to answer the question of the resurrection on a redaction–critical level (i.e. a matter of the editor's intention) rather than on the straightforward historical one. Perrin comments:

Now we no longer ask ourselves, Did Jesus appear as risen from the dead to his disciples not at all (so Mark), or in Galilee (so Matthew), or only in Jerusalem and its environs (so Luke)? Instead we ask ourselves, What is Mark trying to say to us by deliberately omitting appearance stories, or Matthew by locating the major appearance in Galilee, or Luke by limiting appearances to the Jerusalem area?[6]

The basis on which Perrin builds such a redaction-critical solution is, of course, his conviction that the meaning of the post-resurrection appearances cannot be discussed simply on the level of history alone.

So where do we go from here? What should be said in the face of such historical scepticism? Is it true that the question of the meaning of the resurrection accounts can *only* be assessed on the level that Perrin suggests? There is a sense in which Perrin is entirely correct, that the editorial considerations must be taken into account when we consider the resurrection narratives. But does that mean that other considerations are neglected? Two key things need to be said in response. The first is perhaps overly obvious, but it needs to be stated anyway. It may just be that the ending of Mark did contain resurrection appearances, but that these have simply become lost in the process of transmission of the Gospel. Perrin's position is built upon the assumption that Mark never contained such accounts and proceeds to interpret both Matthew and Luke on that basis. In fact, the whole of the 'scepticism' theory is undermined if Mark did originally have a fuller narration of these events. Admittedly, this is an argument from silence on our part, since our best copies of Mark do not contain such accounts of resurrection appearances now. Nevertheless, it is worth making the point clear and at least re-open the door of possibility on this matter.

Secondly, it has to be said that Mark does not omit entirely all references to the resurrection of Jesus within his Gospel.[7] In point of fact, Mark has quite a bit to say about it. There are several key passages which hint at the resurrection of Jesus as a key theme in the Gospel, including the three passion predictions of 8:31, 9:31 and 10:34. In addition, there is the often overlooked verse in 14:28 where Jesus tells his disciples he will be raised and go before them *into Galilee* (see also 15:7). It is the geographical setting of this particular verse which is crucial for our consideration at this point since it leads us straight back to a consideration of John 21. The essential point is that Mark 14:28, Matthew 28:16–20 and John 21 all share a common Galilean setting of at least some of the resurrection appearances by Jesus to the disciples. To put it another way, John 21 becomes important independent evidence for a Galilean post-resurrection appearance of Jesus. This indirectly challenges, or at least undermines, one of the foundational assumptions of a position such as Perrin's, namely, that Mark 16:8 was the original ending of the Gospel. We know from John 21 (and Matthew 28:16:20!) that there were several stories relating Jesus's appearances to his disciples in Galilee, something hinted at in Mark 14:28 (and 15:7). One cannot help but wonder if the lost ending of Mark was a version of the story we now know as the epilogue to John's Gospel.[8] All of this is a roundabout way of saying that John 21 has perhaps almost as much to do with studies of the Synoptic Gospels as it does with the rest of the Gospel of John itself.

Let us turn our attention away from the issue of the geographical setting of chapter 21 and move to a larger consideration of the meaning of the chapter itself. To begin our discussion I would like to draw attention to a story, taken from a contemporary work, which has some remarkable similarities to the epilogue of John's Gospel. The illustration will serve to concentrate our attention on what may be the key theme of John 21.

In Hermann Hesse's powerful fictional novel *The Glass Bead Game,* first published in 1943, we are introduced to an élitist society which is found in the remote province of Castalia. The society prides itself as being the highest embodiment of all that is good and true and noble within the human spirit. Castalia is at the same time an educational establishment and rigorously trains the students who come to live and study there in the fine arts, the most noble of which is playing the Glass Bead Game (a sort of philosophical board game which mystically incorporates all of the fields of knowledge within it). Much of the hypnotic appeal of the book is the way that Hesse paints a picture of the ideal clashing with the real, the search for perfection in the midst of imperfection, and the demands that the quest makes upon human beings. The novel traces the career of one Joseph Knecht, who as a young man comes to study at the schools of Castalia and eventually rises, step-by-step, to become the Master of the Game, the highest and most revered position in the society. Master Joseph humbly accepts the role, knowing that it is such an high honour, and performs the necessary tasks well, setting new standards for discipline and purity of life and leading the whole of the society to even more exalted levels of aesthetic achievement.

Eventually, however, Master Knecht finds that the task is unfulfilling and burdensome. Castalia is isolated and detached from the rest of the world and therefore insular and unresponsive to the very richness of life it purports to define and create and claims to embody. Castalia is in fact a society at war with itself, striving to maintain its ideals in the face of extreme challenges from both within and without. Master Knecht resigns his position as Master of the Bead Game, an unprecedented move, and retreats to private life, taking on the simple role of teacher to a young man named Tito. Joseph is blissfully happy and celebrates his new-found freedom, and fulfilment as a private instructor, by going swimming with Tito in a nearby lake.

Then the unexpected happens, tragedy strikes, and Joseph drowns while swimming. Tito is beside himself and, standing at the lakeside, looking at the place where he last saw his Master, wonders aloud. He cannot imagine how life will go on without Joseph, his mentor, teacher and friend. He blames himself for the death of Knecht, since it had been on his insistence that Joseph joined him in swimming in the lake. The body of the novel then closes with this paragraph in which Tito's thoughts at the death of his Master are recorded:

Oh! he thought in grief and horror, now I am guilty of his death. And only now, when there was no longer need to save his pride or offer resistance, he felt, in shock and sorrow, how dear this man had become to him. And since in spite of all rational objections he felt responsible for the Master's death, there came over him, with a premonitory shudder of awe, a sense that this guilt would utterly change him and his life, and would demand much greater things of him than he had ever before demanded of himself.[9]

I cannot help but think of the scene at the conclusion of the Gospel of John whenever I read this story by Hesse. The similarities are quite remarkable and one cannot but wonder if Hesse had the New Testament passage in the back of his mind when he wrote the novel. Tito recognizes that his life will be irrevocably changed by the death of his Master and that it 'would demand much greater things of him than he had ever before demanded of himself.' Such is the power of true discipleship, discipleship which flows as the natural outcome of a healthy Master/pupil relationship.

Surely this call of discipleship lies at the centre of what John wishes to communicate to us in chapter 21 of the Gospel. Peter must have felt a similar 'pull of the heart' demanded by his relationship to his Master as he stood along the lakeside in Galilee. And yet, in spite of the superficial similarities between the two lakeside narratives, they are in reality poles apart. The irreducible difference between them is, of course, that Peter is talking to a living Master, not merely gazing forlornly, as does Tito, at the lake where his Master has just died. Still, if Hesse can, through a story that is pure fiction, fill us with a sense of wonder about the nature of true discipleship, how much more so can John's Gospel challenge us! Let us examine the chapter a bit more closely.

As I hinted earlier, the focus of the story in chapter 21 is on the disciple Peter and the conversation he has with the risen Christ. The miraculous catch of fish in verses 1–11 almost serves as an introduction to the dialogue between Jesus and Peter. Almost certainly the three-fold call to discipleship in verses 15–17 is related to the three-fold denial by Peter of Jesus at the arrest of Jesus (as recorded in Matthew 26:69–75, Mark

14:66–72 and Luke 22:56–62, although, it must be said, only two denials are described in John 18:25–7).

Let us pose, for a moment, the interesting question: How did this story of Peter's conversation with Jesus come to be part of the tradition of the early Church? Are we able to say anything about why this story was preserved and re-told among Christian believers? We may have an important clue in verses 18–23 where the deaths of both Peter and the Beloved Disciple are discussed in very allusive terms. In other words, it has been plausibly suggested that John 21 was written shortly after the death of Peter, or at least that the desire to honour the recently-departed disciple Peter is partially responsible for the shaping and preservation of the narrative. It makes sense to suggest that Peter's death would be an impetus to recall Jesus's words about his death and formalize them into a written form. The message of the risen Christ in the face of the impending death of his disciple is found in verse 19 and is clear and emphatic — 'Follow me!' Just in case the point is missed, or deflected onto another subject (as Peter attempts to do by asking the question about the fate of the Beloved Disciple), it is re-emphasized in verse 22 — '*You* follow me!' For Peter this call to follow Christ led inexorably to his eventual martyrdom, probably by crucifixion upside-down, if the cryptic meaning of 21:18–19 is so deciphered and Church tradition is to be believed. Surely Peter discovered, as indeed all of us should discover in our own way, that (to echo the words of Hesse) being a disciple of the Master means that greater things will be demanded of us than we ever dreamed possible. Such is the way of the Cross.

NOTES TO CHAPTER 3

1   A study of the process of development undergone by the Gospel of John involves a consideration of the whole of the Johannine corpus, the assumption being that the Epistles of John and the Apocalypse offer some clues as to what the Johannine community, usually thought to be located in Ephesus, believed and taught. I myself basically accept the scheme of development outlined by Raymond Brown in *The Gospel According to John,* Volume 1, transl. K. Smyth (Doubleday, New York, 1966), pp. xxxiv-ix.

2   R. Morgan and J. Barton *Biblical Interpretation,* (Oxford University Press, 1988), p. 54.

3   J.D.G. Dunn *Christology in the Making,* (SCM Press, London, 1980), p. 250.

4   There is some difficulty in knowing precisely what the hymn means to say here. Two possibilities of translation exist, depending upon how one punctuates the sentence in 1:3–4 and how one interprets the participle phrase 'ho gegonen'. The RSV reads: 'without him was not anything made that was made. In him was life...', while giving the alternative as a footnote, 'without him was not anything made. That which has been made was life in him.' Our reconstruction follows the second of these possibilities.

5   George R. Beasley-Murray, *John,* Word Biblical Commentary (Word Books, Waco, Texas, 1987), p. 10.

6   Norman Perrin, *The Resurrection According to Matthew, Mark, and Luke*, (Fortress Press, Philadelphia, 1977), p. 6.

7   The other main witness whose testimony cannot be overlooked is that of the apostle Paul, particularly as he discussed the resurrection appearances in 1 Corinthians 15:3–5. Perrin acknowledges that Paul's witness may ultimately be decisive in settling the matter, but proceeds with his study of the Synoptic accounts without taking into account Paul's contribution. This undoubtedly is a major methodological error on his part and may be described as the 'Achilles heel' of his argument.

8   Although John 21, as it now stands, is clearly a product of the Johannine community, sharing similarities of language and style with the rest of the Johannine literature, nevertheless, at an earlier oral stage it may have been related to the lost ending of Mark 16. Chapter 21 is one of the focal texts discussed within a recent stimulating monograph by Kevin B. Quast entitled *Peter and the Beloved Disciple: Figures for a Community in Crisis*, JSNT Supplement Series 32 (Sheffield Academic Press, 1989). Quast explores the relationship between the two apostolic figures and offers some fresh ideas about the nature of the Johannine community and the place that chapter 21 has in our study of it.

9   H. Hesse, *The Glass Bead Game* (Penguin Books, Middlesex, 1972), p. 395.

QUESTIONS FOR THOUGHT AND DISCUSSION

1.   In the light of the re-use of the hymn in John 1:1–18, can you think of some contemporary ways in which Christianity has taken on the surrounding cultural ideas and popular expressions and used them as an effective way to communicate Christ?

2.   Clarence Jordan has commented on the implications of John 1:14, and the fact that we as Christians are called to embody the truth of Christ's presence in our lives, in this way: 'The Incarnation of Jesus was not a point; it is a process.' Is this a helpful way to understand our responsibilities in the world today? Why or why not?

3.   What is the greatest thing that God has thus far demanded of you in your path as a disciple of Christ?

4.   Examine John 1:1–18 in light of *Wisdom of Solomon* 7 and *Wisdom of Ben Sirach* 24:3–9. What are the similarities? What are some of the differences? How do these compare with Hebrews 1:1–3 and Colossians 1:15–20?

5.   Schuyler Brown, *The Origins of Christianity* (ch.2 n.3 above) p. 108, comments: 'All the gospels must be read on two levels, as narratives of the ministry of Jesus and as reflections of the ecclesiastical contexts in which and for which they were written.' What exciting, new possibilities of understanding does this approach open up with regard to the Gospel of John? What limitations and dangers are there in following it?

IV

Resolution of a Rivalry

What was the relationship between Jesus and John the Baptist? This has been one of the most perplexing problems facing students of the New Testament over the years. Quite clearly, John the Baptist had an enormous impact upon his Jewish and Roman contemporaries. He shook the province of Judaea, in which he lived, in a way that few people ever did, before or since. In addition to the gospel accounts of the Baptist's mission, the fact that sources outside the bible inform us about his challenge to the authority of Herod of Antipas is corroborative testimony to this impact (see Josephus's *Jewish Antiquities* 18. 116–19).[1] Josephus implies that John the Baptist's ministry was perceived by Herod to be extremely disruptive politically and that the King eventually had him executed in about 32 CE, apparently in an attempt to forestall any further trouble.

Yet the question of the precise connection between the ministry of John the Baptist and Jesus has more to offer us than these mere historical facts indicate, if we examine it closely. This is a particularly important matter when we come to John's Gospel because of the special interest that the Gospel has in the figure of John the Baptist. Before we turn to consider some of the specific passages from the Gospel, I would like to begin with a simple illustration, drawn from what might appear to be the most unlikely of sources — a well known TV show.

Gene Roddenberry's imaginative creation *Star Trek* is undoubtedly one of the most popular TV series of all time. It has developed something of a cult following, even among young people who were born long after the original series finished production in 1969. The appearance of a completely new series and (to date) five movie sequels also testify to the popularity of the idea of an adventure series set in outer space. One of the reasons why the series has had such a phenomenal success is perhaps to be found in the way that the two main characters — Kirk and Spock — are portrayed. The individual characters are allowed to develop their own personalities, show strengths and weaknesses, face and solve incredibly difficult (albeit far-fetched) situations, as the stories unfold week by week. The juxtaposition of the logical, Vulcan Spock with the highly emotional and bombastic Doc McCoy has also helped to make the series dramatically interesting and entertaining. And yet, no one ever is left to doubt who is in ultimate charge of the star ship. All decision, all command, falls upon the shoulders of the Captain — James T. Kirk. He is, after all, the main star and has top billing and we have watched him dominate the show week after week. Yet I think it is true to say that the key to the series, its dramatic 'hook', is in the relationship between the two main characters — Spock and Kirk. A good example of this is to be found in a famous episode entitled *City on the Edge of Forever,* (which incidentally won the Hugo Award for Best Dramatic Presentation of 1967). As always, in this episode the crew of the *Enterprise* are faced with a seemingly insurmountable problem that they must solve. In this particular case it is the fact that Kirk, Spock and McCoy are all trapped in the past history of earth, in America during the 1930's, to be exact. They are called upon to save the world from a Nazi victory in World War 2, and the whole of subsequent earth history is dependent upon the way that Kirk decides to act. In this particular episode Kirk and Spock befriend a woman named Edith Keeler and seek her advice and help. She suspects that her guests are from somewhere else and recognizes that they do not fit very comfortably within her world. At one point within the dialogue she makes a perceptive comment about the relationship between Captain Kirk and Spock, as she understands it. Spock asks, 'Where would you estimate we belong, Miss Keeler?' She turns to Spock. 'You?' she answers, pondering for an instant, and then with a nodding gesture towards the Captain she continues her reply to Spock: 'You belong at his side. As if you have always been there, and always will.' The relationship between the two central characters is precisely defined and highlighted by the statement. The Captain is in charge and Spock is assigned the supportive role of First Officer once again. We thereby know who is the leader, and who has the supportive role. Our understanding of the way that the *Enterprise* is run is confirmed, and we all breathe a little easier. The Captain is in control and everything will work out in the end.

I have used a rather simple example to illustrate what I feel to be an essential point about the nature of the relationship between Jesus and John the Baptist. There is a real sense in which John the Baptist, however powerful and charismatic a figure he may have been, belongs forever at the side of Jesus. It is Jesus who is the focal point of the gospel story, not John the Baptist. It is Jesus of Nazareth who must take over the reins of history from John the Baptist, whose task has been to prepare the way for him. From our vantage point two millenia later, this seems crystal clear, without any problem. And yet, the story is not quite that simple and straightforward. There are some residual tensions detectable within John's Gospel over the precise relationship between the two men and their respective ministries. Let us examine some of the key passages a little further.

1. JOHN THE BAPTIST AS ELIJAH RE-BORN

How did John the Baptist conceive his own ministry? How did he view his role and its significance in relation to Jesus? These are not easy questions to answer, at least not without a fairly thorough examination of the New Testament. Perhaps the simplest way to highlight some of the difficulties in answering them is to note the following two Gospel passages side by side:

And the disciples asked Jesus, 'Why do the scribes say that first Elijah must come?' He replied, 'Elijah does come, and he is to restore all things; but I tell you that Elijah has already come, and they did not know him, but did to him whatever they pleased...' Then the disciples understood that he was speaking to them of John the Baptist.' (Matthew 17:10-13)

And this is the testimony of John, when the Jews sent priests and Levites from Jerusalem to ask him, 'Who are you?' He confessed, he did not deny, but confessed, 'I am not the Christ.' And they asked him, 'What then? Are you Elijah?' He said, 'I am not'. (John 1:19-21a)

To put the critical question, 'Was John the Baptist Elijah *Redivivus,* the famous prophet of Ancient Israel living again, or not?' It appears that the very least we can say is that Jesus certainly thought that he was, while John the Baptist was of the opinion that he was not. Admittedly, we have wrenched the two passages from their respective contexts and may find that when examining both more closely the starkness of the contrast is somewhat relieved (perhaps John the Baptist developed in his understanding of his own role). But there remains, nevertheless, some latitude within the New Testament witness about the role that John the Baptist had as the forerunner of the Messiah.

How widespread the idea of an Elijah-like figure coming as a forerunner to the Messiah was within Jewish expectation of the first century is a matter of considerable debate. Eschatological precision was as inexact in those days as it is now and there is much to suggest that Jewish thought on such matters was far from fixed. There was a great deal of speculation in the air, and we may be catching a whiff of it here in these passages.

Indeed, I cannot help but wonder if part of the difficulty surrounding this particular issue is that John the Baptist thought that *Jesus* was the Elijah-figure. In other words, perhaps initially, John the Baptist thought that Jesus was Elijah *Redivivus* and therefore viewed himself as merely a forerunner to the forerunner, so to speak. This would certainly explain why John the Baptist is made to answer in John 1:21a as he does. Certainly in the Synoptic Gospels John the Baptist is praised highly by Jesus as the prophetic figure who inaugurates his (Jesus's) own ministry. Several important passages from various sources within the Synoptics confirm this high opinion of Jesus about John the Baptist. From Mark we should include Mark 6:14-16, 8:28, and 11::30-2 (and parallels in Matthew and Luke); from the source that scholars call 'Q' there are Matthew 11:7-9 = Luke 7:24-6, and Matthew 11:11 = Luke 7:27-8; and from Mathew's special source ('M') there is Matthew 21:31-2. Perhaps the most interesting of these, in one sense, is Mark 6:14-16. Here we see how Jesus is understood by the people to be John the Baptist (Elijah) come back from the dead. Again this is further evidence of the tremendous feeling of eschatological expectancy which pervaded the time.

In any event, there are a few other considerations about the way that John the Baptist is portrayed in the Gospel of John which need to be examined to gain a fuller picture of the place that the Baptist has in his Gospel.

2. A BAPTIST SECTARIAN GROUP

One of the most interesting questions raised by a study of John the Baptist concerns the followers that he undoubtedly attracted. What was their relationship to Christianity? Several key passages from the New Testament witness need to be looked at in an attempt to answer this.

Firstly, we note the two rather suggestive passages in John 3:22–6 and 4:1 where we can detect vestiges of a rivalry between disciples of Jesus and disciples of John the Baptist. Apparently the disciples of John the Baptist were somewhat put out by the fact that Jesus's ministry was attracting more followers and that Jesus and his disciples were performing more baptisms (How modern! The homiletical potential of this point alone is vast!). This rivalry is perhaps not so surprising when we recall that some of Jesus's first followers were in fact originally disciples of John the Baptist himself (as 1:35–7 states). Nowhere does the human spirit raise itself up more vigorously than when an ego is bruised, and it appears that some of the disciples of John the Baptist, at least, were worried about the affrontery of the 'Jesus' group. Some scholars have taken 4:2 to be a corrective statement inserted by a later editor to challenge the assertion that Jesus himself baptised, a correction which stands as further indirect evidence of the baptismal controversy itself. The question of baptism was certainly a controversial one in those days, but it was not the only sore point.

Another brief glimpse of a rivalry between the disciples of John the Baptist and the disciples of Jesus is to be found in Mark 2:18 (compare the parallels in Matthew 9:14 and Luke 5:33), this time focusing on the issue of fasting. Here the disciples of John the Baptist, now supported by the Pharisees, are contrasted with Jesus's rather lax disciples. The underlying implication appears to be that the fasting disciples are more spiritual as a result of their practices. Yet, John the Baptist answers any such disputes, which could easily give way to a divisive rivalry, in terms of a very firm ranking structure; he places himself in a subordinate role to Jesus. John 3:20 thus becomes the classic formulation of John the Baptist's approach to his ministry: 'He must increase, but I must decrease.'

This is not to say that the influence of John the Baptist disappeared or that his disciples were automatically enrolled as Jesus's. It is true that the cryptic verses in John 10:40–2 do seem to suggest that following John the Baptist's death Jesus visited the area of the Jordan where the Baptist conducted his ministry and found that many of his followers did transfer their allegiance to Christ. However, we get the impression that this was an exception rather than the general rule while Jesus was still engaged in his own ministry on earth.

There are, after all, several passages which testify to the abiding impact of John the Baptist upon the first-century world long after Jesus himself had passed from the earthly scene. We read, for instance, in Acts 19:1–7 of a group of followers of John the Baptist whom Paul encounters in Ephesus and who are led by the apostle to a fuller understanding of the Christian faith. Surely the fact that disciples of John the Baptist are still around thirty years (or so) after their founder was executed, in a distant city nearly 800 land miles away, stands as some witness to the impact of the man.

At the same time, the way in which John the Baptist's witness is described in John 1:6–8 has often been taken to indicate something of a rivalry between Jesus's followers and those of John the Baptist. Here John the Baptist is emphatically declared not to be the light, but merely a witness to the light. One is tempted to read behind the lines and wonder why the idea that John the Baptist is the light is being so emphatically denied. Is it not because some had seen him in precisely this way? I am tempted to think so. Similarly, in John 1:15 we have John the Baptist declaring, in no uncertain terms, the fact that Jesus is pre-eminent over him. Why is this being so strongly asserted? Is it not because there were some who wished to place John the Baptist in the limelight, to exalt him (and his undeniably dynamic ministry) above that of Jesus? Again, I am tempted to think so. In short, are we seeing something of an underlying tension within John's presentation of John the Baptist about the nature and character of his ministry? Almost certainly this is the case.

The only question that is left open is whether the debate about the relationship between Jesus and John the Baptist is to be set wholly within the time of Jesus and John the Baptist or not. Another possibility is that the rivalry is to be set in a later time, perhaps when the author of the Gospel was writing and facing a resurgence of a group of Christians who wished to idealize the person and ministry of John the Baptist. This is precisely what Barrett means when he comments: 'John's rewriting of the synoptic material...may have been due in part to a desire to counteract an excessive veneration of the Baptist.'[2] In all probability it was a little of both; excessive veneration of John the Baptist was almost certainly a problem during Jesus's own day *and* within the later church period as well. John the Baptist was so powerful a prophetic figure, so magnetic a personality, that he would attract followers to him long after his death.[3] It is not too difficult to imagine that this occasionally presented problems within the growing Christian movement in subsequent years.

To return to the *Star Trek* illustration for just a moment, it is humorous to note that in spite of the fact that Spock throughout the series was always given the supportive role to that of Captain Kirk, he was far and away the most popular character of the show. Letters flooded the offices of the TV company demanding that Spock be allowed to take over since he was so much more competent than the all-too-human Kirk. People were attracted to him in such numbers that he was written into more and more episodes to satisfy popular demand. They did not care so much about Kirk, and were more interested in the 'right-hand man'. Even now there are those who are ardent devotees of Spock, in spite of the fact that he was supposed to be only the *Enterprise's* second-in-command.

It does not require too much effort to imagine the disciples of John the Baptist getting a little bit restless over what they judged to be the comparatively feeble preaching of Jesus when they were used to the fiery style of their own heavy-duty leader. Perhaps it is just such a phenomenon that the writer of the gospel of John has to counter within his own setting. It is not strange how consistent human nature is in such matters? The power of the charismatic or unusual personality often wins the day.

3. SOME LESSONS ABOUT EXERCISING CHRISTIAN MINISTRY

We have spent some time examining the New Testament witness concerning the role of John the Baptist. But I want to turn now to consider some of the lessons we might learn from John the Baptist about how we can conduct our own ministry today, whether as pastor of a church or as a leader in the congregation. In some ways I think that John the Baptist should be designated the 'Patron Saint of Pastors'. He certainly embodies a self-effacing attitude toward ministry that needs to be emulated today, especially when we live in a society in which pressures to succeed and claw our way to the top are so great. It is far too easy to focus attention on the messenger at the expense of the message he or she is called to proclaim. Personality cults are easily born and flourish well in our age. There is no doubt that the cause of Christianity has been dealt an extremely damaging blow by high-profile ministers who have not heeded the example given by John the Baptist and who could stand to learn some valuable lessons from him. Ministers are particularly susceptible to the temptations of such personality cults given the very nature of their vocation, the fact that they are in the front line, daily engaged with very human problems and difficulties. The temptation to become the fount of all wisdom and authority is all around us, and the trap is easily fallen into. We all know, sadly, examples of ministry that is conducted in such a way that genuine pastoral concern quickly becomes a disguised personality cult in the worst, repressive, almost Stalinist, tradition. So what lessons can be drawn from the example of John the Baptist? I would like to suggest two here, although undoubtedly there are many others that could arise from the story.

First, there is a lesson concerning the proper way to achieve wholeness and satisfaction in ministry. For John the Baptist the lesson came in the form of being willing to take a lesser role, to take a back seat, for the sake of the larger concerns of the Kingdom of God. Submission is the key here, the realization that in order to win you must surrender.

This is in fact quite a deep-seated New Testament principle. We could say that the principle of mutual submission is the ground of any distinctively Christian ethic. It is the quality which should characterize our whole approach to Christian living. Submission is certainly something which dominated the whole of the ministry of Jesus Christ, who chose to surrender voluntarily to the cross rather than call upon all the angelic forces at his disposal and avoid the cruel death facing him. We could go so far as to say that it is rooted and grounded in the very nature of God, in that God surrenders himself to the 'indignity' of the incarnation and thereby gains the salvation of the whole of humankind.

It is also a principle that we see in operation in the larger world in which we live. On a political scale, real victory, as the military historians tell us, often comes in the form of surrender. Who would doubt that the economic recovery of Japan in the post-1945 era is partly a result of the fact that the nation surrendered to Allied forces in August of 1945, and was thereafter provided with immense amounts of financial support to aid her recovery? Japan now enjoys one of the highest standards of living in the world- and has the admiration of most other countries. There is a very real sense in which the vanquished have in fact become the victors, at least in so far as sheer economics is concerned.

As another simple illustration drawn from life we could note the way in which some of the martial arts are built upon the idea of victory through submission. Judo, for instance, is not so much a purely 'aggressive' sport, as it is a refining and disciplining of physical responses. This is so much so that judo could be more properly described as an art form rather than a 'style of fighting'. It involves learning how to roll with the thrust of your opponent, how to use your weight and centre of gravity most effectively, how to convert your opponent's energy to your account. Through a deft move the person being acted upon turns the opponent's aggression to his advantage, surrendering to it, so to speak, and making the physical forces involved work to his advantage. Thus the most successful masters of judo are not brute 'aggressors', and are rarely the largest or strongest participants in any given contest. Instead, the champions are those who are most able to put this principle of victory through submission into operation within the arena of a physical contest.

This principle of submission needs to be carefully cultivated within the very fabric of our ministries. It is not always easy to achieve. But it is always worth working for, in spite of the difficulties. An example from our life at the college in which I teach might help illustrate the point.

At Regent's Park College we have quite a mixed community of teaching staff, students, and domestic staff. There are people from all age groups and backgrounds, all living together on the college site. One of the regular features of the college life is chapel service on one night a week. As must be the case with every Baptist church in Britain today, we have tensions within the college community over the style of worship that is to be adopted on these evenings. Some prefer to have only hymns sung which are chosen from the Baptist Hymn Book. Others prefer to sing choruses and more modern, up-to-date songs. Some want organ accompaniment and others want guitars and flutes. Some raise their hands during the singing while others prefer to keep their hands by their side. Over the years we have found that the only positive way to resolve this sort of tension is for all of us to agree that if something is found to be really disruptive to others, if some style of worship is actually offensive to another segment of the community, then we would agree not to pursue it. In short, we have had to learn to surrender to each other on such matters. The exciting result of this conscious act of surrender has been that the college fellowship has been significantly enriched and deepened, and our worship was taken on genuineness. That is not to suggest that all of the tensions on matters of chapel worship have disappeared. In point of fact, we would be quite worried if they had simply evaporated in this way, for it would register apathy and resignation rather than concern. But it is to suggest that we are much more conscious of other segments of the community than we had been before and that is a very positive thing. This first lesson of submission as the path of victory is being learned, practised, and its truth vindicated day-by-day by the more positive atmosphere of worship we have come to share.

Second, there is also for us within the example of John the Baptist a lesson concerning timing, a lesson about being appropriate to the task at hand, finding the correct time to introduce God's word to any given situation. This is perhaps one of the most difficult lessons for a dynamically prophetic figure, such as John the Baptist, to learn. Is this not the primary reason why John the Baptist has to send his disciples to Jesus and ask about the progress of the movement which he had helped to inaugurate? In Luke 7:19–23 (the parallel is Matthew 11:2–6) we have John the Baptist sending his disciples to query Jesus about the very nature of the Kingdom of God. Are things progressing according to plan or not? Far from this story as representing a 'crisis in John's faith in God', I rather suspect that this passage is better understood as a helpful glimpse into the very human situation of John the Baptist as he struggles to accept Jesus's timetable. We wonder if John was frustrated by the feeling that he could do things better, or more effectively, or with greater impact, than Jesus was doing them. The answer Jesus gives to John the Baptist's question is quite revealing: 'Blessed is he who keeps from stumbling over me.' Clarence Jordan has remarked that this is the 'Forgotten Beatitude' and suggests an alternative translation that seems more to the point: 'Blessed is the man who does not get upset by the way that I do my business.'[4]

Quite honestly, I do not think that John the Baptist ever learned to accept this vital truth easily. I rather suspect that he struggled with this all his life, and in that way he is very similar to many of us. We too find it extremely hard at times to accept the timing of anyone other than ourselves. In this respect the figure of John the Baptist becomes an object lesson for us.

It is sometimes easy to become so captivated by the rightness of the message we have to proclaim, so convinced by what we have to say, that we may forget the audience that we are addressing and not recognize the needs of the people as they themselves perceive them. There is, after all, at times a vast difference between the *perceived* needs of a congregation, or individual, and their *actual* needs. The wise and experienced pastor is able to address the latter without neglecting the former, for to do otherwise is to risk losing his congregation altogether.

Or, alternatively, we may simply not recognize that our congregations are not able to accept a particular point at that precise moment. In such instances, the lesson to be learned is one of patience and reliance; not that our message must be forgotten or endlessly adapted to the situation so that it becomes void of any real content and loses its biting edge. But the key is to blend proper exhortation with a due measure of pastoral sensitivity and care. Certainly people need to be challenged from the pulpit. But crushed with a harsh word from the privilege of the pulpit? Never! It is wholly inappropriate and damaging to the living Body of Christ. We must be careful that in the rush of enthusiasm and eagerness to proclaim God's truth that we do not end up doing more damage than good.

We would do well to examine our own ministries and ask ourselves how effectively we have learned these vital lessons of submission and timing. They are not all that unrelated, since both have a certain vision of God as their foundation. He submits in divine humility to his creation, freely calling us to partnership with him; but he is still able, in due time, to fulfill his purposes for us. And it is precisely because of the assurance of.his humble love for us, that we can submit ourselves wholeheartedly to him.

4. A MEDITATIVE POEM ON JOHN THE BAPTIST

Finally, I would like to close this chapter with a meditative poem by Eddie Askew on the person of John the Baptist.[4] The poem is based upon the passage in Matthew 11:2–6 alluded to above, the story of John's sending disciples to Jesus in an attempt to get clarification about what was happening with the Kingdom of God. Some of the themes of this chapter are bought out very well by this poem.

Lord, I feel for John.
It must have been tough.
He was used to a hard life,
but that was in the sun and the wind.
Not in a prison cell.
No sweet-smelling violets there!

But worse,
the powerful memories of you.

And now, the painful questions.
Doubts.
His own identity at stake.

'Are you the Messiah?'

Or was it wasted time?
One brief flame of hope
burning his fingers.
Leaving ashes, drifting, on the wind.
Ending painfully.
I know you were close to him, then.
As ever. Standing near.
I hope he knew it.

Lord, I'm grateful
that I, too, have a place
in your design.
I have to admit
I hope it won't end
like John!
But it's good to be involved.
Committed.
And when it falls into place
it feels great.

Sometimes, though, it isn't easy
to see where I fit in.
I feel I'm working in a vacuum.
Nothing connects.

I can't see my place in your plans.
Lord, your purposes go way beyond my horizon.
I can only look back to yesterday.
I can only see ahead to tomorrow,
and not that clearly.
Eternity's a bit big for me,
I've not grown to fit it, yet.

Lord, when I'm puzzled,
uncertain,
help me remember
you're in control.
Your finger on the button.
And, whether I can see the end or not,
help me accept
that you know where we're going.

NOTES TO CHAPTER 4

1   The record of Josephus contains a significant amount of extra detail about the John the Baptist/Salome episode and is thus an important source for filling out the fateful events surrounding Herod's party.

2   C.K. Barrett, *The Gospel According to St. John* (ch. n.6 above) p.171.

3   There exists to this day in the area of Iran/Iraq a Gnostic sect known as the Mandaeans who have, as one of their characteristics, an active devotion to the teachings of John the Baptist.

4   A translation offered by Jordan in a taped bible study from 1968.

5   *Many Voices, One Voice,* (Leprosy Mission International, London, 1985), pp. 11–12.

QUESTIONS FOR THOUGHT AND DISCUSSION

1.   Compose a list of similarities and differences between the preaching of John the Baptist and Jesus. Is it true to say that Jesus's preaching was characterized by grace and John's by judgement?

2.   What would you consider to be danger signs of a developing 'personality cult' within your congregation (it may not necessarily have the pastor as its focus!).

3.   In what ways does the meditation about John the Baptist echo your own thoughts about ministry? Do you ever feel that you have simply wasted your time? Or that you don't really know in which direction you are heading?

4.   The following story is related by Herman A. Hoyt in *My Favourite Illustration,* compiled by Carl G. Johnson, (Baker Book House, Grand Rapids, Michigan, 1972), pp. 60–61: 'During

the Reformation in Europe, Luther and Zwingli found themselves at odds in their concern for the movements they were leading. Early one morning Zwingli walked out on the mountains of Switzerland and a soul-stirring sight confronted him. He saw two goats making their way over a narrow path on the mountain. One was ascending the trail, the other descending. He also noticed that they must pass at a point where the trail was so narrow that there was room for only one goat. He watched to see what would happen. The animals rounded a turn in the path which brought them in full view of each other. They backed up, as though ready for a lunge, and then the most amazing thing happened. The goat on the trail below laid down in the path, while the goat above him walked over his back. The first animal then arose and continued his journey up the trail. To Zwingli this meant that the way down is the way up, which is the course that Christ took. He humbled himself so that men could walk over Him into the kingdom of light, knowing that afterward He would be exalted.' Is this a helpful illustration to demonstrate the nature of Christian humility? What are its strengths and weaknesses?

V

Eternal Life

According to Mark 1:14–15 the first words of Jesus's public ministry were, 'The time is fulfilled, and the kingdom of God is at hand; repent, and believe in the gospel.' The meaning of these words has been the subject of one of the most important and far-reaching debates in the history of the interpretation of the New Testament. Two key features of this discussion have been the meaning of the phrase 'the kingdom of God' and the temporal significance accorded to 'is at hand' (in Greek the perfect verb 'ēngiken' is used). The debate has not been easily resolved, but something of a consensus has been reached on these two foundational matters. Let us briefly summarize the major points of this general agreement.

1. THE PROCLAMATION OF THE KINGDOM OF GOD

With regard to the meaning of the phrase 'the kingdom of God', it is now recognised that this was the burden of the preaching and teaching of Jesus. That is to say, that the proclamation of the coming of the 'kingdom of God' formed the substance of Jesus's ministry on earth. All of his teaching in parables, his miracles of healing, his ethical instruction to the disciples, revolves around this central idea of the 'kingdom of God', much as in the physical world the planets in our solar system revolve around the sun. But what precisely does the phrase mean? To repeat an oft-asserted distinction, the 'kingdom of God' is primarily a theological statement of the rule or reign of God and not a statement about God's realm as a geographical area. For those of us who live in the United Kingdom this mental disassociation of 'kingdom of God' from any particular location is perhaps a little more difficult to manage. We must struggle against it all the time. In order to get away from the geographical associations of the term, Clarence Jordan[1] translates the Greek phrase as 'the God Movement', something which communicates the dynamism of the idea much more powerfully to us today in a world filled with 'movements' of all sorts.

We could perhaps best illustrate the fact that 'reign of God' or 'rule of God' is closer to Jesus's message by calling attention to the petition within the Lord's Prayer (as recorded in Matthew 6:10). There Jesus teaches his disciples to pray: 'Thy Kingdom come! Thy will be done on earth as it is in heaven.' Remembering the Aramaic fondness for using parallel doublets in prayer (the fact that a second line is often given to clarify and expound the meaning of the first), we have in effect a ready-made definition by Jesus of what it means for 'the kingdom of God to come'. It is any place where 'the will of God is done on earth as it is in heaven.' This understanding of the 'kingdom of God' in terms of the reign or rule of God in human affairs has been one of the most important results of scholarly investigation into the Gospels during the past century or so.

Second, with regard to the timing of the coming of the 'kingdom of God', the critical question is: *when* does the kingdom of God come? Again, scholarly debate has raged over this particular issue and a commonly accepted answer has been slow to emerge. Nevertheless, it is now generally accepted that Jesus's message concerning the timing of the kingdom was that it has a present dimension as well as a future one. That is to say, that in and through Jesus's own life and ministry the kingdom had already come, but that its future fulfilment was yet to be awaited. The New Testament thus contains what has been described as an 'inaugurated' eschatology (where 'eschatology' means thinking about the last things of life and history); it presents a 'now/not yet' understanding of the kingdom of God. For this reason, George Eldon Ladd has described the 'kingdom of God' as 'The Presence of the Future' and actually so titled his book on the subject.[2]

To be honest, it is extraordinarily difficult for us to grasp the truth of this realized/future tension within the New Testament and good illustrations to help us conceptualize it are hard to come by. Perhaps one of the most popular has been the D-Day/V-Day illustration offered a number of years ago by Oscar Cullmann.[3] The point, quite simply, is that just as there was a delay between the events of June 6, 1944 and the final collapse of Germany in May of 1945, so, too, is there a delay between the inauguration of the 'kingdom of God' by Jesus and its ultimate consummation, which is still awaited.

A second illustration that some have found helpful is that of the game of chess. Those who play the game professionally, or at least with some proficiency, are able to guage the progress of a match with a fair degree of accuracy. There comes a critical point in each contest — it may even be identifiable in a single move by one of the players — after which the final outcome of the match is determined. It is simply a matter of allowing the rest of the moves to be made, to let the game run its course. This is why chess championships very rarely are played to check-mate; such a thing is unnecessary since both players know what the outcome will be already. There may be an exchange of rooks or knights that has not been plotted beforehand, but who the final victor will be is known long before the end comes. So, too, we could say that the winning move of the 'chess-game' of the kingdom of God has already been made in the person of Christ. It is just a matter of allowing time to run its course.

Another helpful, non-militaristic illustration is that of parenthood. There is a real sense in which an expectant mother and father are, for the duration of a first period of pregnancy, neither completely childless nor truly parents. They live in the gap between parenthood and non-parenthood, a sort of 'parental twilight zone'. Yet, the effects of the imminently awaited child are all around them and can readily be seen. Physiological changes take place in the mother; both mothers and fathers may suddenly become quite broody and act somewhat irrationally as they adjust psychologically to the idea of being parents. Their attitudes and expectations about the future begin to be altered to accommodate the baby which is to come. For them, life in the present is being shaped by an event which is yet to come in the future. No expectant parent can act as if life is exactly the same as it was before news of the pregnancy came to light. The baby, although not even born yet, is in a very real sense dictating the actions and attitudes of the parents.

In just such a way does the 'presence of the future' kingdom of God affect our lives now, even though the ultimate fulfilment is awaited sometime in the future. This is the profound message of the New Testament concerning the 'kingdom of God'. Yet, John's particular way of expressing this tremendous truth needs to be examined in more detail.

2. TRANSPOSITION INTO ANOTHER KEY

We noted in chapter 1 that this characteristic idea of Jesus's ministry, the proclamation of the kingdom of God, does not find much expression in John's Gospel. John uses the phrase 'kingdom of God' only in 3:3 and 3:5. Instead, John's tendency is to discuss the burden of Jesus's preaching and teaching in terms of 'eternal life'. Here we encounter one of the most important Johannine emphases, one of his most distinctive theological truths. It is as if to say that Jesus's declaration about the kingdom of God has been absorbed by the idea of 'eternal life', and all that it encompasses, within the Gospel of John. John has, to put it another way, transposed the 'kingdom of God' into another key, that of 'eternal life'. The essential 'music' is the same, but it is heard with new harmonies.

But we are still confronted by a problem of definition. What is meant by the phrase 'eternal life'? Quite clearly John means not just 'life that goes on forever'. It is not just a matter of the length of life that is at stake here. This whole notion of 'eternity' is, once again, a very difficult concept to grasp, since we as temporal human beings generally find conceptualizing about time beyond our limited capabilities, outside of our realm of experience. It is no wonder that Einstein's theory of relativity remains a closed book to most of us, even at the most elementary of levels. It is extremely difficult for us to imagine time in any other way than in straightforwardly chronological, or 'horizontal', terms. We may find that our thoughts are perfectly reflected in the words of one young girl who writes a letter of inquiry to God:[4]

> Dear God
>
> Can you tell me what forever is
> because no one else can?
>
> Mary

To pursue Mary's question: What is 'forever'? More to the point for our considerations, what does John mean when he uses the expression 'eternal life'? These are important questions which get right to the heart of the New Testament witness concerning our hope and our faith. Yet they are extraordinarily 'slippery' concepts and we often use language about them very imprecisely. Perhaps an additional illustration taken from the ancient world will help us appreciate the meaning of 'eternal' a little better.

The ancient Latin legends of the *Sibyl* help illustrate what a burden sheer longevity of life can be. Ovid's *Metamorphoses* 14:132 relates the story of the young Sibyl with whom the god Phoebus has fallen in love. Phoebus wants to marry her, but she is reluctant and unsure. In an attempt to bribe her Phoebus offers the Sibyl anything that she wishes. The Sibyl points to a heap of dust which had been swept together from the floor and asks that she might have as many birthdays as there were grains of dust. Her wish is granted, but she discovers that it becomes a tremendous curse, since she forgot to ask for perpetual youth as well. Instead of having happiness extending far into the indefinite future, the Sibyl discovers that her longevity becomes an awful thing to bear, a mockery of life. Her eternal life lived on a purely temporal scale is not a blessing at all, but an unending damnation for her. She is condemned to thousands upon thousands of years as a sunken, shrivelled, old hag, her beauty lost, her friends a forgotten memory, her daily tasks a dreary, unending monotony. Death itself is but an illusive dream; the Sibyl must live on and on with no release in sight. T. S. Eliot makes just this point in the Preface to his poem, *The Waste Land* (1922): 'For once I saw with my very own eyes the Sibyl at Cumae hanging in a cage, and when the boys said to her, "Sibyl, what do you want?", she answered, "I want to die."' The Sibyl discovers, all too late, that there is also something about the *quality* of life which must help define the very meaning of 'life' itself.

John seems to be pointing to this essential truth via his use of 'eternal life'. By it he means a qualitatively different type of life, life that is lived on a different level. We could say that he means life in another, deeper and more spiritual dimension, that it is life on a 'vertical' level.[5]

Or, to put it another way, 'eternal life' is life that is lived in all its fullness, because it is conciously lived with an eye to God himself. John recognizes that real life is spiritually determined and uses this rather curious phrase 'eternal life' as a shorthand expression for this. As John has Jesus declare in 10:10, 'I have come that you might have life, and have it more abundantly.' By the phrase 'eternal life' John means that life itself needs always to be defined in terms of its relationship to the Giver of Life. We have 'eternal life' because it is part of our relationship with the one who is himself eternal. And because it is life that flows from our relationship with the eternal God, it carries on beyond the boundaries of this mortal existence. Death, far from being a terminus, is, in Christian terms, a doorway into another fuller dimension of life. Yet, paradoxically, something of that fuller dimension of life can also be experienced and felt in the here and now.

We move on now to consider some of John's special ways of describing the significance of 'eternal life' and all that it means, for Christian believers. This is a vast topic and there has been a virtual flood of books, articles, and essays written over the years on this feature of Johannine theology and it is impossible to do justice to them all here. We can but point to one or two of the most interesting examples within our study here. First, we consider John's use of the pregnant phrase 'the hour'.

3. 'THE HOUR' OF GOD'S POSSIBILITIES MADE REAL

The phrase 'the hour', or 'my hour', is a very important one within John's Gospel, with the noun itself occurring some 25 times. It is not only a marvellous window into the nature of the Christian experience as John understands it, but also an important way of seeing the Johannine presentation of Jesus's understanding of his own mission. Thus, it is intimately linked to John's concept of 'eternal life' and to his concept of 'salvation'. Ralph Martin has commented on the phrase that it 'can be traced throughout the Gospel of John (2:4; 7:30; 8:20; 17:1; 19:25–7), which suggests [it is] a literary key to the Gospel. The evangelist pinpoints Jesus's time before and after his 'hour', and the structure of the Gospel conforms to this single idea.'[6] Let us examine the phrase more closely. There are three specific things to be noted about its appearance in the Gospel.

First, we note that 'the hour' is something which Jesus himself awaited during his ministry. Several passages highlight this point. For instance, in John 2:1–11 we have the story of Jesus attending the wedding at Cana along with his disciples. In the midst of the celebrations Jesus's mother comes to him and points out that the wine reserves have been depleted. The setting for the miracle that follows is thereby established. Jesus replies to Mary in very polite, but somewhat detached terms, 'Oh woman, what have you to do with me?' Then he adds the critical, explanatory phrase 'My hour has not yet come.' It means that Jesus was awaiting some decisive time to arrive before he would reveal himself. This is why he is reluctant to get involved in the situation at the wedding at Cana. The timing was not yet right.

We find exactly the same thing related twice more in John's Gospel. In chapter 7 Jesus is embroiled in a controversy with some Jewish leaders at the Feast of the Tabernacles in Jerusalem. The Jewish leaders get so angry at Jesus that they try to arrest him. John then records in 7:30 that they were unable to do so 'because his hour had not yet come.' Similarly, in chapter 8 another confrontation between Jesus and the Jewish religious leaders is said to take place in the Temple precincts. John notes in 8:20: 'but no one arrested him, because his hour had not yet come.' Quite clearly, there is a strong note of anticipation with regard to the decisive 'hour' in these three passages. But do we know when this decisive hour was to arrive? Do we have any clues as to its identity? In order to answer this we move to consider the second way in which 'the hour' is used in John's Gospel.

Next, we note that 'the hour' is, above all, something that Jesus endures in his passion. Here we see a close connection between 'the hour of Jesus's death' and the 'time of his glorification'. That is to say, that the impending hour of Jesus's death is, ironically, also the hour of his glorification. In and through Jesus's death the glory of God is made manifest. Several passages serve to highlight this point. In 12:23–4 we have a prediction of Jesus's passion recorded by John. Jesus says: 'The hour has come for the Son of Man to be glorified. Truly, truly, I say to you, unless a grain of wheat falls into the earth and dies, it remains alone; but if it dies, it bears much fruit.'

Just a few verses later, in 12:27–36, we see Jesus struggling with his own impending death and agonizing in prayer before his disciples and the father.[7] In 12:27 Jesus prays: 'Now is my soul troubled. And what shall I say? "Father, save me from this hour"? No, for this purpose I have come to this hour.' Finally, in 13:1 the idea surfaces again with John commenting that before the Feast of the Passover 'Jesus knew the hour had come to depart out of this world to the Father'. The close association this 'hour' of departure has to the theme of glorification of the Father through the Son can be further seen in 13:31–2 where Jesus declares: 'Now is the Son of man glorified, and in him God is glorified; if God is glorified in him, God will also glorify him in himself, and glorify him at once.' The same thing holds true for 17:1 where Jesus emphatically declares: 'Father, the hour has come; glorify the Son that the Son may glorify thee.'

Finally, we note that 'the hour' is used in a few select passages of John's Gospel to communicate something about the life we as Christians presently experience in Christ. It is here that we see John's realized eschatology coming to the fore most clearly. Three passages are particularly important for this point. We shall consider each briefly, highlighting the realized element contained within each saying by placing it in italics.

The first passage to be considered is found in 16:32, where Jesus is talking to his disciples and remarks: 'The hour is coming, *indeed it has come,* when you will be scattered, every man to his home, and you will leave me alone; yet I am not alone, for the Father is with me.' Jesus is here picking up the theme of persecution of the disciples which is hinted at earlier in the chapter and described as a 'coming hour' (16:2). This reference in 16:32 may appear at first to be a slightly unusual way to emphasize our life in Christ since it concentrates so heavily on our failure to persevere and stay by his side. But the context is hardly one of pervading despair or sadness, for Jesus goes on to declare in the very next sentence that, in spite of tribulations and trials the Christians are not to despair because, as Jesus puts it, 'I have overcome the world.' The resounding note of victory comes through, even in the face of treachery and betrayal on the part of the disciples.

A second passage, more to our point, is found in 4:23 where, in the course of Jesus's conversation with the Samaritan woman, he states: 'The hour is coming, *and now is,* when the true worshippers will worship the Father in spirit and truth, for such the Father seeks to worship him.' The realized emphasis is clear and unmistakable here. Jesus is saying in no uncertain terms that the true believer has already entered into the realm of the eternal.

The same essential idea is also brought home in 5:25 during Jesus's discourse with the Jewish leaders on the nature of the resurrection and its connection with his identity as the Son of God. Jesus there declares: 'Truly, truly, I say to you, the hour is coming, *and now is* when the dead will hear the voice of the Son of God, and those who hear will live.'

One further question needs to be asked at this point. Are we to take all of these sayings about 'the hour' to be accurate reflections of the very words which Jesus spoke in Aramaic? Some of the relevant passages are clearly editorial explanations (such as 7:30; 8:20 and 13:1) and we can put those aside for the moment. But some of the statements about 'the hour' are presented in John as declarations made by Jesus himself. Are they the actual words of Jesus or are they added afterwards in light of the Church's experience of the risen Christ? This is not an easy question to answer and it has been one of the most debated focal points in recent years. What seems the best way forward?

In most instances it is perhaps best to take these 'realized' references as having been added later to the oral traditions of things that Jesus actually said, which were preserved in the Christian community. That is to say, that the author of the Gospel, under the inspiration of the Holy Spirit, is updating the words of Jesus so as to reflect the present experience of the believing community. This is perhaps the best way to understand 4:23; 5:25; 16:32. (For further explanation of this approach, see pages ??-?? above.) Having said that, one or two of these 'hour sayings' may indeed be actual words of Jesus, particularly those which emphasize his hesitancy about performing 'signs' because the time had not yet arrived (such as in 2:4), and his predictions about the disciples suffering persecution (such as in 16:2,4).

We turn now to consider a related passage, one which stresses that Jesus's death on the cross is also a statement about the judgement of Satan.

4. LIFTING UP TO GLORY: JOHN 12:30-33

In chapter 1 we mentioned in passing that the motif of 'glory' has a central place in John's Gospel, serving as a focus for John's message of God's redemptive action in and through Jesus Christ. That is to say, that in Jesus Christ we see the 'glory' of God most clearly revealed (as is explicitly stated in 1:14b). The same motif of 'glory' is developed elsewhere in the Gospel; often it is used almost as a means of linking together other key theological ideas. Sometimes the actual word 'glory' need not even be used, but the ideas associated with 'bringing glory to God' make it plain that this is what John wishes to communicate.

Nowhere is this more clearly seen than in 12:30-3, where the idea of Christ's death is closely connected with the idea of judgement of Satan, or to use John's way of describing him, the 'ruler of this world'. In effect the crucifixion of Christ is the judgement upon Satan. In this passage the key word 'glory' does not appear, but another suggestive way of communicating the 'glory of God' idea is used. In verse 32 Jesus declares: 'I, when I am lifted up from the earth, will draw all men to myself.' How do we move from this cryptic description of the crucifixion–judgement to the idea of 'glory'?

G.R. Beasley-Murray has called attention to the verb 'hupsoō' in 12:32 and the fact that there is a close relationship between the Aramaic verbs meaning 'to crucify' and 'to exalt' (the conceptual overlap of the two being best expressed in English through the verbal expression 'to lift up'). Beasley-Murray says in this connection: 'The Evangelist's concern in using the term 'hupsothenai' appears to be to emphasize the unity between the death on the cross and the ascent to rule. The key to it is the eschatological action of God in and through the Son of Man whereby his 'lifting up' becomes his installation to sovereign rule.'[8] Several other key New Testament passages draw together the ideas of Jesus's death and his exaltation to glory, notably the hymns of Philippians 2:6–11, Hebrews 1:3 and 1 Timothy 3:16. The fact that all of these passages are probably hymnic fragments dating from the earliest period of the early Church suggests that Christ's crucifixion was very early on seen as also an elevation to glory.

The strength of this association of ideas is that it links together 'judgement–crucifixion–exaltation–glory' in a way which seems to get right at the heart of John's theology of the passion. To put it another way, the crucifixion of Jesus Christ was certainly a physical raising up of the Lord, but it was at the same time an exaltation of him to glory, as well as a judgement upon the 'ruler of this world'. To return to the task at hand: How does all of this affect the Christian and his possession of 'eternal life'? Of what relevance is it?

The connection is quite straightforward: if the crucifixion of Jesus Christ stands at the same time as the point at which Satan has been judged, then the Christian believer is free fom his (Satan's) power. Judgement upon 'the ruler of this world' has already been effected and the Christian is free to enjoy the 'eternal life' which flows to him or her as a result of belief in Christ. John stresses this point in a variety of passages, including 3:17–18: 'For God sent the Son into the world, not to condemn the world, but that the world might be saved through him. He who believes in him is not condemned; he who does not believe is condemned already, because he has not believed in the name of the only Son of God.' 5:24: 'Truly, truly, I say to you, he who hears my word and believes him who sent me, has eternal life; he does not come into judgment, but has passed from death to life.' Thus, we see clearly how in Johannine thought the crucifixion of Jesus is seen as a 'glory-filled' event, one which has tremendous implications for the lives of the believers, since it is also the act of their deliverance from evil and the channel of their entry into eternal life.

Finally, we turn now to consider one more feature of John's realized eschatology, his account of Jesus's words from the cross. Here, once again, we see that a powerful theological statement is being made, through John's use of the story of Jesus's passion, about the realities of the Christian life in the present.

5. 'IT IS FINISHED!'

In chapter 1 we had occasion to discuss the tendency to harmonize the life of Jesus and blend together the four Gospel accounts. Perhaps nowhere is this more clearly demonstrated than through the way in which the sayings of Jesus from the cross have often been treated. In fact there are 7 so-called 'sayings from the cross' recorded within our New Testament. But it sometimes comes as a surprise to discover just how these seven sayings are distributed. Consider the following table:

1. 'My God, My God, why have you forsaken me?'
   (Mark 15:33/Matthew 27:46)

2. 'Father forgive them, for they don't know what they are doing.'
   (Luke 23:34)

3. 'Truly I say to you, today you will be with me in paradise.'
   (Luke 23:43)

4. 'Father, into your hands I commit my spirit.'
   (Luke 23:46)

5. 'Woman behold your son... Behold your mother.'
   (John 19:26–27)

6. 'I am thirsty.'
   (John 19:28)

7. 'It is finished!'
   (John 19:30)

The first thing to notice is the fact that the sole saying recorded in both Matthew and Mark is the same, probably due to Matthew's reliance upon Mark for the passion narratives in his Gospel. This means that if the only Gospel we had were Mark (or Matthew, for that matter), we would have quite a different picture of the crucifixion itself. The only statement of Jesus is one of extreme dereliction, of forsakenness and isolation. The effect is to heighten the theological meaning of the gospel story, emphasizing the cross as the place where Jesus shares the consequences of human sin.

However, the sayings that Luke records for us give us a slightly different picture of the crucifixion. Here we see Jesus demonstrating his compassion to the criminal on the cross next to him, pausing in the midst of his own pain and anguish to offer some words of comfort to a fellow execution victim. Jesus also prays for those responsible for his death, both Jewish leaders and Roman officials alike, in another noble act of selfless love. In contrast to the cry of dereliction we saw in Matthew and Mark, here in Luke it is a cry of submission and supreme trust that comes forth from Jesus's lips. Luke's narrative gives us a rather different insight into the meaning of the cross.

When we come to John, however, an even more interesting picture emerges. There is, as in Luke, a characteristic concentration of Jesus upon others with the statements made to Mary and 'the disciple' (presumably the Beloved Disciple) about mutual responsibility. The second saying from the cross recorded in John is usually taken to reflect John's fight against a 'docetic' interpretation of the gospel story, that is one which tried to deny the full humanity of Jesus. John, so the argument goes, wishes to stress that Jesus had real human needs and physical desires including thirst. Perhaps there is something to be said for this, but it is important to note that all of the Synoptic gospels record the offer of wine on a sponge, although none of them record the saying about thirst which John does (Matthew 27:48; Mark 15:36, Luke 23:36).

The most important saying from John for our consideration is the final one, 'It is finished!'. The Greek for this is a single word, 'tetelestai'. It is a perfect passive verb, the force of which is somewhat difficult to translate into English, but something which should be examined closely since it is highly significant theologically. We must remember that the force of a perfect verb in Greek is action that has been completed in the past but which still continues to be felt in the present. It is as if Jesus declares in 19:30: 'The act of redemption has been completed by my death, and it stands forever completed.' The effects of that 'finishing', that 'completion' are still being felt, the results still valid for all Christians in succeeding generations. Once we give the perfect verb its full force we can easily see how this saying of Jesus from the cross is at the same time another way for John to emphasize his realized eschatological viewpoint. Eternal life has come in the life of the believing Christian because the act of redemption has been completed and still stands completed. John Calvin put it this way: 'Now this word of Christ is most memorable, for it teaches us that the whole accomplishing of our salvation and all the parts of it are contained in His death.'[9]

In short, we experience salvation now because of what was accomplished ('tetelestai') on that crude, wooden cross nearly two thousand years ago. Is there a greater mystery? It is difficult to conceive of one.

NOTES TO CHAPTER 5

1   As in his *Sermon on the Mount,* Revised edition, (Judson Press, Valley Forge, Pennsylvania, 1976).

2   G. Eldon Ladd, *The Presence of the Future* (Eerdmans, Grand Rapids, Michigan, 1974). This is a revised and expanded version of an earlier book by G. Ladd entitled *Jesus and the Kingdom* (1964). Another important book on this whole subject is G.R. Beasley-Murray's *Jesus and the Kingdom of God,* (Paternoster Press, Exeter, 1986).

3   The illustration is found in a number of Cullmann's writings and has been picked up by a number of other writers. A good example of its use is found in *Christ and Time,* (SCM Press, London, 1951), p. 84. The sermons of Karl Barth are also an excellent source for other practical illustrations of this 'now/not yet' tension which lies at the heart of Christian faith. See, for instance, *Deliverance to the Captives,* (Harper, New York, 1961), pp. 149–50. Barth's *Dogmatics in Outline,* (SCM Press, London, 1949), pp. 122–3, should also be consulted.

4   Taken from *Dear God, Most of the Time You're Quite Nice,* compiled by Maggie Durran, (Fount Paperbacks, London, 1985), p. 103.

5   John uses the word 'zoe' 36 times in his Gospel, always distinguishing it from mere biological life.

6   Ralph Martin, *New Testament Foundations*, Volume 1, (Eerdmans, Grand Rapids, Michigan, 1975), p. 272.

7   This is the Johannine equivalent to the Garden of Gethsemane episode which is recorded within the Synoptic Gospels (Matthew 26:36–46, Mark 14:32–42 and Luke 22:39–46). Luther comments on the Gethsemane episode: 'No one feared death like this man!'

8   'John 12, 31–2: The Eschatological Significance of the Lifting up of the Son of Man', in *Studien zum Text und der Ethik des Neuen Testaments, Festschrift zum 80 Geburtstag von Heinrich Greeven*, edited by Wolfgang Schrage, (Walter de Gruyter, Berlin, 1986), p. 73. The same interpretation is offered, with less technical detail, in his *John, Word Biblical Commentary*, (Word Books, Waco, Texas, 1987), pp. 214–15.

9   *Calvin's Commentaries: The Gospel According to St. John 11–21*, edited by David W. Torrance and Thomas F. Torrance, (Saint Andrew Press, Edinburgh, 1961), p. 183.

QUESTIONS FOR THOUGHT AND DISCUSSION

1.   Many of your congregation may be able to remember the events of D-Day/V-Day. Ask them to share with you some of the feelings that they had during this 'interim period'. At what stage did they become convinced of total victory? What lessons does this teach us about the nature of the 'kingdom of God'?

2.   Compare the story related in Numbers 21:4–8 with the statement made in John 12:30–2. What similarities are there? Do you think that John may have had this story in mind when writing chapter 12?

3.   John 19:30 declares that 'It is finished!' In what ways is the Christian life one which is characterized not by a sense of completion, but a sense of expectation? What is yet awaited?

4.   On a personal level, what things would you like to see God still do within your life? Within the life of your family? Within the life of the congregation you serve?

5.   Prepare a Lenten sermon series based upon the 'Seven Sayings from the Cross'. How could you bring out the distinctive perspectives of each of the Gospel writers through the saying or sayings he has recorded?

VI

The Paraclete

In the last chapter we concentrated our attention on the idea of 'eternal life' as it is expressed in John and thus sought to come to a better understanding of the 'realized eschatology' contained within the Gospel. In this chapter we turn to a closely related topic — John's concept of the Holy Spirit. We could put the connection between the two ideas in the form of a question: *how* does the Christian believer experience this 'eternal life' here and now? The answer comes in John's Gospel, at least in part, through his distinctive doctrine of the One who is called the Paraclete. In other words, to put the matter on an individual level, we could say that the Christian enjoys eternal life because of the presence of the Paraclete within his or her life. To make the same point on a more corporate scale, we could say that the Church experiences the gift of salvation because the Paraclete has been sent to her from God the Father, and from Jesus.

This might lead us to think of the Paraclete as being synonymous with the Holy Spirit as described elsewhere within the biblical witness, such as in Romans 8. But does such a simplistic equation of the Paraclete with the Holy Spirit get to the heart of the matter? How accurate is it? Certainly we should affirm that the Johannine idea of the Paraclete is closely related to his understanding of the Holy Spirit. The two overlap considerably in John's mind. That much is clear and no one would dispute it. But are the two ((Holy Spirit and Paraclete) completely interchangeable? In order to answer this more fully, we need first of all to examine the sayings about the Paraclete which are contained in John's Gospel. Before we do that, one final point needs to be made about the importance of such a discussion in the present ecclesiastical climate.

It seems undeniable that 'Holy Spirit' and 'Paraclete' are particularly topical subjects considering the developments within our churches in the last twenty years or so. In recent years within the British church scene as a whole, there has been a resurgence of interest in what might be termed 'Holy Spirit matters'. We are enjoying a rediscovery of the spiritual dimension to our faith, a refocused concentration on activities often said to be prompted by the movement of the Holy Spirit amongst God's people now. [1] 'Charismatic renewal' movements have brought much needed life into many flagging congregations; of that there can be no doubt.

At the same time. we have to note that there have also been the inevitable excesses all such religious movements seem to carry with them. The tendency to cater to extreme subjectivism must be checked or the 'renewal' is wasted, lost, or becomes positively counter-productive and divisive for the Body of Christ. This essential truth has been demonstrated over and over within Church history, from the church at Corinth in the 50's CE, through the Montanist controversy in the second century, through the highly-charged millennarian movements of the Reformation, and so on right up to the present day.[2] Any casual examination of church history will reveal that this is so, and we should not flatter ourselves to think that what we experience today is something completely new. Nor, on the other hand, should we think that what is taking place today is altogether unimportant. Our task is to accept all that is good and healthy in such spiritual renewal movements, without losing our critical faculties which enable us to recognize the all-too-human weaknesses and limitations embedded within them.

This means that the teaching and guidance provided by John's Gospel concerning the Paraclete is as important now as it has ever been, since it helps us gain a biblical perspective on such matters. John's teaching about the Paraclete provides us with an important basis upon which to discern spiritual renewal within the church. Yet, John may surprise us, and perhaps challenge us, by the manner in which he describes these matters of the Spirit, since he does so in such 'Jesus-centred' terms. John's startling revelation is that Jesus himself will send 'another Paraclete' (14:6) to the disciples after he is finally gone and returned to heaven. That is to say, that this is how he (Jesus) will be experienced by them, how he will come back to them from the other side of death. Thus, the Paraclete could be said to be the indwelling presence of the Spirit of Christ within the life of the church. In some ways this is not the approach we might have expected.

One of Noel Coward's most popular and enduring plays is the comedy-farce *Blithe Spirit*. In it the story is told of a writer, Charles Condomine, and his wife Ruth, a fairly happy couple who live in relative comfort in the Kentish countryside. The play relates how, during the course of one late-summer weekend, the couple find their comfortable lives greatly disrupted by the return of the departed ghost of Charles's first wife Elvira. She had been dead for several years and the passing of time had caused Charles's memory of her to become somewhat idealized. However, the arrival of Elvira on the scene wreaks havoc in the household, causing a great deal of tension and friction between Ruth and Charles. Tempers flare, the furniture of the house is thrown about and destroyed, accusations and innuendoes fly as a result of this ghostly appearance. Eventually this visitation from beyond the grave drives poor Charles to wish that the spirit of Elvira had never appeared at all. He discovers how chaotic her return could be, what tremendous disruptions it can cause, and wishes that things would return to normal; but of course they never can.

On a superficial level, we might be tempted to see the play as a parable about much of the disunity and division that has been caused in the life of the church in recent years. There is undoubtedly much that has gone on under the guise of the activity of the Holy Spirit, or the manifestation of the Paraclete. It is not difficult to imagine church situations where we too might be tempted to wish that the 'charismatic extremes' had never taken place, that this latest manifestation of the spirit had never happened, that life could continue normally as before. And yet, where would the Church be without this gift from above? Where would we be without this manifestation of the presence of the Risen Lord in our midst? When it is put that way, the tensions and difficulties which arise out of an over-emphasis on the Holy Spirit begin to take their proper place.

We now turn to examine more fully those passages which speak of the Paraclete within the Gospel of John. Following this, we shall turn to consider two related matters which arise from a careful consideration of the Johannine doctrine of the Holy Spirit/Paraclete.

1. THE PARACLETE SAYINGS

There are five passages in John in which the Paraclete is described: 14:16–17; 14:26; 15:26–7; 16:7–11 and 16:13–15. The noun 'paraklētos' also is applied to Jesus in 1 John 2:1, something which links together the Epistle and the Gospel as both belonging to the same tradition, often called 'the Johannine School'. Some, on the basis of this 'Paraclete' concept, have argued that the author of the Gospel is therefore also the author of the Johannine Epistles.[3]

Beyond these few brief references, there are no other statements about the Paraclete as such, and thus it stands as an exclusively Johannine motif. Furthermore, one of the striking things about the concept of the Paraclete in John's Gospel is that it is wholly contained within the so-called 'Last Supper' discourse of chapters 13–17. This fact in itself has inevitably led to scholarly discussion about whether the Paraclete sayings are a post-resurrectional description made within the Johannine community of her experience of the Risen Lord Jesus. It certainly is very striking that the Paraclete sayings are grouped together into such a very specialized section of the Gospel, one which is almost exclusively concerned with discipleship matters and most probably reflects the later Johannine community. D. Moody Smith[4] remarks that in chapters 14–16

[Jesus] speaks to the post-resurrection church. The problems addressed are distinctively and explicitly Christian. Jesus, by the device of describing in advance the future situation, addresses the present existence of Johannine Christians, and so the present Christian moment or dimension of the Fourth Gospel emerges in complete clarity.

Rudolf Schnackenburg makes the same essential point with these words:

Within the framework of the farewell discourses, the sayings about the Paraclete have the primary function of encouraging, admonishing, and consoling the community by promising the Spirit or by reminding the members of that community that they possess the Spirit. They can only carry out that function if the promise is in accordance with the community's living experience of the Spirit.[5]

In short, it seems we cannot avoid the conclusion that the doctrine of the Paraclete in John is very much an ecclesiastical one; it arises from the church's attempt to interpret her life in light of the central fact of Jesus Christ's resurrection, and to express her experience of 'eternal life' in the here and now. That is where we must begin if we are to understand the meaning of these few references to the Paraclete within the Gospel of John.

However, in spite of the limited number of references to the Paraclete in John there is a diversity of meaning and function assigned to him (while we shall use the masculine personal pronoun for the Holy Spirit throughout, I do not intend thereby to attribute any gender to the Spirit of God). This means that 'Paraclete' yields a rich harvest of theological meaning. For instance, there are statements about the steadfastness of the Paraclete (14:16 — He will be with you forever); his teaching role (14:26 — He will lead you into all truth); his role as witness (15:26 — He will bear witness to Christ); his role as judge (16:7 — He will convict the world concerning sin, judgment and righteousness); and his role as guide (16:13 — He will guide you into all truth). In short, we have in the Johannine doctrine of the Paraclete a rich vein of theological wealth.

All of this serves to illustrate one of the main difficulties we face when we come to grasp John's presentation of the Paraclete. It has to do with the fact that the term 'Paraclete' is an extremely difficult one to translate; at least it is difficult to find a single English word which can function as its equivalent and convey all of this diversity of meaning. There is such a diversity of role and activity associated with the 'Paraclete' in John that we run the risk of missing some of it if we insist rigidly on a single, equivalent term. For instance, it is often pointed out that there is a close connection between the Greek word 'paraklētos' and the Latin term 'advocatus', and that the primary meaning of 'Paraclete' is therefore a legal one ('one who stands beside you in a trial'). While this is certainly one idea associated with the term 'Paraclete', it is by no means the only one. Nor does the forensic terminology exhaust the meaning of 'Paraclete', as the descriptions of the Paraclete as teacher (14:26), guide (16:7), and judge (16:7) all indicate. In short, we must recognize the novelty of the Johannine term 'Paraclete'. We could almost say that in John was clearly seen the 'invention' of a new term to describe the Church's experience of the risen Lord Jesus Christ.

A similar problem of language was faced in the ancient world by one of the most talented and ambitious Roman military leaders the world has ever seen — the young Octavian. Following the victory of his armies and navies over those of the rival Mark Anthony at the battle of Actium in 31 BCE, Octavian was confronted with the age-old difficulty of propagating not only news of his conquest, but also his part in the institution of the so-called *Pax Romana* which followed. How was he to proclaim his triumphs abroad and let the world know of his achievements? Several honoured and esteemed titles were common within the Roman world and were picked up and used to this end by the Octavian camp, including 'Imperator', 'Son of Caesar' (harkening to the fact that he was the adopted son of the murdered Julius Caesar), and 'Triumvir'. Yet, Octavian eventually decided that these titles and descriptions of him were insufficient to the task at hand, since they did not make it clear that a completely new dimension had entered into the Roman political scene, that a revolutionary new era had begun. So in 27 BCE Octavian coined a new term and applied it to himself, the title 'Augustus'. It evoked just the right associations of national and religious order as well as military might and power. The title became so closely identified with Octavian and his rule that we no longer even know him by his old name, but universally describe him by this new title. Effectively it becomes his very name, and we all but forget the name 'Octavian' in our history books.

Similarly, the Johannine community has created, adopted (perhaps from Jesus?), or at the very least developed substantially, this new term, Paraclete. The community does so to describe the new era that the Church has entered, the new experience of the Risen Lord Jesus which has begun. The term 'Paraclete' stands as a crucial expression of this relationship with the Lord Jesus. This prompts us to consider in what ways the whole idea of the 'Paraclete' is related to the person of Jesus Christ himself.

2. JESUS AND THE PARACLETE

One of the most extraordinary features of the Paraclete sayings as they occur in John is the fact that they duplicate other statements about Christ which are contained elsewhere in the Gospel. There is virtually nothing that is said about the Paraclete in terms of his function and role that is not said elsewhere about Jesus Christ. Several examples spring to mind to illustrate this, notably the passage in 14:15–21 which juxtaposes the Paraclete and Christ on many key points. Note the following three examples drawn from this paragraph alone:

1. 'I [Jesus] will come to you' (14:18)
   'He [Paraclete] will come to you' (14:16)

2. 'The world will not receive me [Christ]' (14:19)
   'The world will not receive him [Paraclete]' (14:17)

3. Jesus will dwell in the disciples (14:23)
   The Paraclete will dwell in the disciples (14:17)

The fact that Jesus promises to send to his disciples 'another Paraclete' prompts the question: Why 'another'? Who was the first? The answer must surely be that the first 'Helper' (or however we choose to translate 'Paraclete') is Jesus himself. The unity of 'Paraclete and 'Jesus' in the Gospel of John is an absolutely fundamental point.

Just to highlight it further we need to mention one additional feature about the concept of the Paraclete/Holy Spirit as contained in John — the fact that it is linked to another key idea — the crucifixion of Jesus on the cross. Earlier, in chapter 5, we noted how Jesus's death is presented as a divine manifestation of the glory of God. The lifting up of Jesus on the cross was at the same time a supreme revelation of the exaltation that belongs to him as the Son of God. We see how John's ideas about the 'Paraclete' are themselves attracted to this central focus of the cross when we remember that Jesus's last words in 19:30 are accompanied with the statement that 'having hung his head, he handed over the Spirit'. The Greek is quite suggestive here, omitting any reference to the spirit as belonging to Jesus (in the sense that it is 'his life', or 'his spirit', that is intended). Instead the sentence includes the definite article ('he handed over the Spirit') and leaves the reader wondering about whether this was deliberately intended as a piece of double meaning. Who within the Johannine community could have ever read this or heard this and not recognize that it is deliberately intended to invoke thoughts about the Paraclete? It is hard to imagine that the attentive listener or reader would have missed the nuance. One further illustration of this is seen in the saying by Jesus recorded in 7:38 about rivers of living water flowing out of the believer. The very next verse has the writer of the Gospel explaining the significance of the statement of Jesus by relating it to his Spirit/Paraclete concept. John 7:39 reads: 'Now this he said about the Spirit, which those who were to believe in him were to receive; for as yet the Spirit had not been given, because Jesus was not yet glorified.'

All of this is a shorthand way of saying that the Paraclete doctrine in John is very much an extension of Johannine christology. The idea of the 'Paraclete' revolves around a christological axis, finding that as its centre. We best understand the 'Paraclete', not so much as an expression of Johannine *pneumatology* (his understanding of the Holy Spirit), but as an expression of Johannine *christology* (his understanding of Jesus Christ). It is, of course, extremely important in this regard to make sure that we are not imposing later credal formulations about the persons of the Godhead and the nature of the Trinity upon the Gospel of John (more about this in a later chapter). To do so means that we lose one of the most important characteristics of the Gospel — the fact that the Paraclete is so closely linked to the person and work of Jesus himself.

We could go so far as to say that the doctrine of the Paraclete in John is certainly not a substitute for his understanding of the Holy Spirit; to equate the two is to miss the subtlety of John's thought. But the Paraclete might be said to be a bridge between Jesus and that transcendent reality which we would now call the Spirit of God, or the Holy Spirit. A Trinitarian understanding of the Holy Spirit certainly cannot be directly deduced from John's Paraclete doctrine, although one can easily appreciate how the Johannine idea of the Paraclete lends considerable support to such a later formulation of faith and belief. One final matter demands our attention.

3. THE JOHANNINE PENTECOST: JOHN 20:22

One of the most perplexing verses to interpret in the whole of John's Gospel is 20:22. Here we find the risen Lord Jesus sitting and talking with his disciples, presumably in the Upper Room. He offers them what proves to be his final, intimate blessing, breathes on them, and utters the words 'Receive the Holy Spirit'. Sometimes this act is known as the 'insufflation' of the disciples by Jesus, calling attention to the Greek verb translated 'he breathed on them'.[6] The basic consideration is whether this passage is intended by John to be his equivalent to the Pentecost episode as recorded in Acts

2:1–4. That appears to be the inference contained in the first stanza of the hymn of Bianco de Siena (died 1434), which is translated in our hymn books thus:

> Come down, O Love divine,
> Seek Thou this soul of mine,
> And visit it with Thine own ardour glowing;
> O Comforter, draw near,
> Within my heart appear,
> And kindle it, Thy holy flame bestowing.

It seems clear that within this hymn we have a Johannine reference to the 'Comforter' being blended with the language of Acts 2. But is this passage in 20:22 really John's version of the Pentecost? If it is not, what is its relation to Pentecost?

Several related questions arise out of this critical verse in 20:22. Some have seen the command 'Receive the Holy Spirit' as a symbol or metaphor of each and every Christian's spiritual life. Others have interpreted the whole episode of 20:19–23 as a pre-Pentecost anointing of the Spirit upon the disciples by Jesus. Some have argued that it was an experience that was unique to the original apostolic band and one that was not repeated ever again (the implication of this is that it is the events of Pentecost which relate the outpouring of the Spirit upon the Church as a whole). Some have interpreted 20:22 as though it were an 'embryonic Pentecost', a proleptic version of what came to be experienced later in the life of the Church. Others have taken this last point one step further and have gone so far as to suggest that the reception of the Holy Spirit in the life of the modern believer comes in two distinct stages: one paralleling the Upper Room insufflation, and a second, subsequent, blessing paralleling the Pentecost episode. This idea has tremendous repercussion upon any theology of 'Spirit-baptism' as based upon the New Testament texts. What shall we make of all this?

The first thing that needs to be noted is the fact that there are indeed many parallels between the 'insufflation episode' of John 20:22 and the Pentecost episode as recorded in Acts 2. These parallels are not to be dismissed lightly, particularly if we enlarge the comparison to include the second story of Jesus's appearance in John 20:24–9 and the introduction to Acts contained in 1:1–8.

For instance, in John 20:19 we are told that the disciples are gathered into one place, with the doors shut, when Jesus appears to them. This is similar to the statement in Acts 2:1 that on Pentecost the disciples 'were gathered into one place.' In 20:25 (and 20:27) Jesus offers his hands and sides to the disciples (and to Thomas) for examination as proof that he has risen. This echoes Acts 1:3 where the author tells us that Jesus 'presented himself alive after his passion by many proofs'. Similarly, Acts 1:8 records the fact that the disciples will become witnesses throughout the regions of Judaea and Samaria and elsewhere after they have been filled with the Holy Spirit. This recalls 20:21 where Jesus mentions his own sending of them into the world just as the Father sent him. The comment about forgiveness of sins contained in 20:23 is also very similar to that found in Acts 2:38, with the added connection being that the gift of the Holy Spirit is expressly linked to this promised gift of forgiveness. In short, there are a number of striking parallels between the Pentecost episode in Acts 2 and the final discourse between Jesus and his disciples as recorded in John 20:19–29. But is this enough to sustain the idea that John is providing us with an alternative Pentecost? In order to move toward an answer on this we need also to consider the parallels between John 20 and Luke 24.

The similarities between John 20 and Luke 24 are in some ways even more striking than those of John 20 and Acts 2. Not only are there recorded comments about the forgiveness of sins and the sending out of witnesses in Luke 24:47 which parallel those already noted in John 20 and Acts 2, but there are several other key phrases and ideas as well. For instance, the declaration made by Jesus to the disciples, 'Peace be with you' in John 20:26 has an exact, word-for-word parallel in Luke 24:36. Likewise, the description of Jesus as 'standing in the midst of the disciples' (John 20:19) is paralleled by Luke 24:36. If that is not enough, the fact that Jesus displays his hands and feet to the disciples, and chides Thomas for his disbelief, finds similar expression in Luke 24:39. Even the note of the disciples' joy is common (John 20:20 and Luke 24:41). In short, we find that the story of Jesus's meeting with the disciples in the Upper Room recorded in John 20 has close connections with both the immediate post-resurrection appearances of Luke 24 and the subsequent Pentecost episode described in Acts 2.

These observations lead us toward the conclusion that in John's Gospel the narrative contained in chapter 20:19–29 is, at least in part, the Johannine equivalent to Pentecost. Has Jesus returned to the Church in the person of the Paraclete? Is this how we are to interpret such statements as 14:18 where Jesus says 'I will not leave you desolate. I will come to you.'? Is his 'coming' to be equated with the 'giving of the Paraclete' and left at that? Certainly we cannot deny that Jesus has indeed come in the person of the Paraclete, but how does that affect a belief in his final climactic appearance ('parousia') at the end of time, his Second Coming? It is not hard to see how the Johannine doctrine of the Paraclete has been associated in some people's minds with a move away from the literalness of the Second Coming of Christ. Such an idea, it is suggested, has been superseded by the events of the Paraclete, to use John's language (or Pentecost, to use Luke's). Jesus has indeed returned to the church, but he has done so in the person of the Paraclete. Is this a proper reading of John's Gospel?

In my mind such an interpretation of the doctrine of the Paraclete as found in John might be described as committing a classic error. It is right in what it explicitly affirms, but wrong in what it implicitly denies. It is correct insofar as it affirms the continuing presence of Jesus in the life of the church through the Paraclete, but misleading in that it denies the consummation of the Lordship of Jesus at his final appearing ('parousia').[7] It has to be doubted whether the Johannine community would have seen the former as necessarily ruling out the latter. At the same time, however, it is true that there is not the same sense of futuristic apocalypticism within the Gospel of John as there is within the Synoptic Gospels on this point. The clearest statement akin to Mark 13, and its parallels in Matthew and Luke, is found in John 14:1–4, and that has lost much of the apocalyptic imagery and character contained in the Synoptic passages. Or, we could put the matter more positively and say that the abiding influence and presence of the Paraclete within the Johannine church is so strong, and so real to them that it colours how the future expectations of Jesus are perceived and expressed. The presence of the Spirit/Paraclete does not eliminate future hopes; that would be to take the matter too far. But it certainly does curtail and modify them and inevitably shifts the focus of attention to a present, realized eschatology.

This is the conclusion reached by a number of New Testament scholars who have wrestled with these very complicated matters of a Johannine realized/futuristic hope and a Spirit/Paraclete concept. One of the most exhaustive studies of the subject has recently been completed by Gary Burge. He comments: 'The resurrection is not spiritualized nor the *parousia* lost. On the contrary, John's chief concern is to show how these two events have direct implications for the believer's present experience . . . The climax of the gospel is the believer's personal experience of Jesus.'[8] This personal experience of Jesus Christ that the believer enjoys is, of course, another way of describing the effects of the indwelling of the Paraclete himself.

We close this chapter with a prayer written by Karl Barth[9] for Pentecost Sunday. Note within it the declaration about the abiding presence of the Paraclete in the life of the believing community of faith.

O Lord, our God, we come before Your face, bowing before Your majesty in recognition of our unworthiness and giving thanks for all Your good gifts which You give us again and again for body and soul. We thank You especially for this Sunday and Holiday, in which we may ponder the fact that Your dear Son, our Lord Jesus Christ, did not leave us orphaned after His return to You, but desired to be and remain present for us in the Holy Spirit, the Comforter and Teacher who makes us alive, until He Himself returns in His majesty. And now grant that we may know You aright and praise You aright in this Your blessing to us, that Your word may be proclaimed aright and heard aright in this place and everywhere Your people call on You. Hallow and bless our celebration of the Lord's Supper, as we share in it with one another. May Your light enlighten us! Your peace be among us! Amen.

NOTES TO CHAPTER 6

1   James D.G. Dunn has written extensively on the relationship between Jesus, the Holy Spirit and the charismatic movement, offering a sound interpretation of the relevant New Testament texts while paying particular attention to the contemporary Pentecostal tradition. Of special note is his *Jesus and the Spirit: A Study of the Religious and Charismatic Experience of Jesus and the First Christians as Reflected in the New Testament,* (SCM Press, London, 1975).

2   For an interesting survey on this matter, produced by the Society of Pentecostal Studies, see: *Charismatic Experiences in History,* edited by Cecil M. Robeck, (Hendrickson Publishers, Peabody, Massachusetts, 1985).

3   On this subject, see: C.H.Dodd, *The Johannine Epistles,* Moffatt New Testament T Commentaries, (Hodder & Stoughton, London, 1946), pp. xlvii–lvi.

4   D. Moody, Smith, *John,* Proclamation Commentaries, (Fortress Press, Philadelphia, 1976), p. 44.

5   R. Schnackenburg, *The Gospel According to St. John,* Volume 3, transl. D. Smith & D. Kon (Burns & Oates, Tunbridge Wells, 1982), p. 153.

6   This very same Greek verb is the one used in the Septuagint of Genesis 2:7 where God breathes life into Adam (humankind). The theological significance of the parallel should not be overlooked; Jesus is breathing life into a new humanity just as God did into the first man.

7   It is not until the writing of Justin Martyr (c. 100–60 CE) that we find the *parousia* discussed in terms of a 'first coming' and a 'second coming'.

8   Gary Burge, *The Anointed Community: The Holy Spirit in the Johannine Tradition,* (Eerdmans, Grand Rapids, Michigan, 1987), p. 147. This is an excellent study by a student of Professor Dunn's and should be consulted by anyone who wishes to explore the matter further.

9   Karl Barth, *Selected Prayers,* (John Knox Press, Richmond Virginia, 1965), p. 45. Slightly emended.

QUESTIONS FOR THOUGHT AND DISCUSSION

1.   The Greek word 'paraklētos' in 14:16 is translated in a variety of ways by scholars and translation committees. Note the following:

     New American Standard, Good News, Mofatt — 'Helper'
     The Jerusalem Bible, New English Bible, Weymouth — 'Advocate'
     Knox — 'He who is to befriend you'
     Revised Standard Version, New International Version — 'Counsellor'
     Tyndale, Authorized Version — 'Comforter'
     Phillips — 'Someone else'
     Schonfield — 'Advisor'
     Raymond Brown, G.R. Beasley-Murray, R. Schnackenburg — 'Paraclete'

Which do you prefer and why? Why do you think that the last three scholars have decided simply to transliterate the word?

2.   Raymond Brown, *The Gospel According to John,* Volume 2, (Doubleday, New York, 1970), p. 1141, poses the following question: 'What brought the Johannine tradition to put emphasis in the Last Discourse on the Spirit as the Paraclete, that is, as the continued post-resurrectional presence of Jesus with his disciples, teaching them and proving to them that Jesus was victorious and the world was wrong?' The answer, Brown suggests, is two-fold: the passing away of apostolic eye-witnesses and the delay of the *parousia* of Christ. How does this suggestion help us understand the function of the Paraclete in the context of an early Christian community? In the context of our own communities? Are there similarities?

3.   Suppose someone in your congregation came to you and said, 'You may be a Christian, but unless you have been filled with the Spirit like me, and like the believers at Pentecost, you are not living in the fulness of the Christian life.' How would you respond? How might John's Gospel be of use to you in your reply?

4.   Gary Burge, *The Anointed Community* (n.8. above) pp. 223–4, says: 'John 20:22 serves not only as a fulfilment of the Paraclete promises but as the climax of the Gospel itself: Christ brings himself to his followers in a coalescing of images from the resurrection, Pentecost, and the parousia.' Do you agree?

5.   Consider the following statement by George Appleton on John 20:19–23: 'Once Christ has been lifted up on the cross the world mission can begin. On the evening of the day of resurrection, the Risen Lord sends his disciples forth with the gospel of forgiveness. He knows that they will have hardships and difficulties to face, so He breathes into them His own victorious Spirit.' Is our reception of this 'victorious Spirit' reflected in our mission activity?

VII

Sacramentalism in the Gospel

We now turn to consider the question of sacramentalism within the Gospel of John, by which I mean the way that the acts of baptism and Lord's Supper are presented in the various stories and discourses of the book. Once we begin to examine the Gospel account closely, we see that there are a great many hidden references to both baptism and the Lord's Supper; hardly a chapter passes by without at least one or two allusions to them appearing. Yet, it must be said that nowhere in the Gospel of John is there an *explicit* reference to either the Christian practice of baptism or to the Christian celebration of the Lord's Supper. What we have are a number of veiled hints about these sacraments as they came to be practised in the Church.

Having made this disclaimer we must also go on to state that so prevalent are these 'sacramental hints' that we cannot help but be drawn to the conclusion that they form an integral part of Jesus's message as transmitted to us through John. Thus, Etienne Charpentier comments that, 'The celebration of the sacraments — baptism and eucharist — often crops up in this Gospel. It is there in the last resort that the words and actions of the earthly Jesus make sense.'[1]

But what is the intended Johannine teaching about the 'sacraments'? In order to gain a perspective on this, we need to go on to ask a related question: How closely is the sacramental question related to the purpose of the Gospel of John itself? It is in attempting to answer this question that a study of baptism and Lord's Supper in John is most revealing. It is also a prime illustration of how differences of opinions can arise over how to interpret key passages in the Gospel.

The place that both baptism and the Lord's Supper have within the Gospel of John has been a matter of considerable dispute. It is striking how divided scholarly opinion on this particular matter is. Here, perhaps as in no other single area of Johannine theology, we have diametrically opposing interpretations being offered for exactly the same passages. Some wish to argue that the writer John is conducting a campaign arguing for a greater sacramentalism in the Johannine community, holding forth many instances of sacramental language and imagery as a convenient focus for the faith of the community, a nodal point for them to gather in unity and harmony. Others have argued for exactly the opposite case, saying that the writer John is wishing to correct what he feels is an over-emphasis on such sacramentalism, pointing them instead to a true faith which does not rely upon such outward, human expressions.

A word of caution must be interjected here. It would be too easy to dismiss this debate as essentially one arising purely from our own perceptions and presuppositions about the place that both baptism and the Lord's Supper have within our present-day denominations. But the truth of the matter is that it is not simply Anglo-Catholic and Roman Catholic scholars who wish to argue for a sacramental interpretation of John. Nor is it true that Baptists and Presbyterians and others in the Reformed tradition always argue against such a sacramental interpretation. It is possible to find devout and well-intentioned interpreters on both sides of the theological fence, arguing for what we might think is the unexpected viewpoint, given the ecclesiastical tradition of the writer concerned. For instance, John Fenton, a Canon of Christ Church, Oxford, has recently offered some cautions against an over-sacramental interpretation of John. He says, for example, in connection with the Bread of Life discourse in John 6:1–71 that:

John has [written] in protest against what he sees as the misuse of sacraments; they can be turned into objects and things in such a way that the personal relationship between Christ and the believer is obscured and forgotten. John's whole enterprise in writing his book may be seen as an attempt to prevent this from happening.[2]

Why is there this diversity of opinion? I think that one of the reasons for this is precisely because we are discussing something which is central to the very message and purpose of the Gospel of John, and to the Christian faith itself. It is precisely because of its importance that sacramentalism has become one of the most discussed topics in Johannine studies. We are here discussing the relationship between the inward belief of our faith and its outward expression, and nothing is more needed in today's world than clarity about how we can openly and publicly demonstrate our faith in Jesus Christ to the world in which we live, as well as encounter God through the materials of that same world (bread, wine, water). For this reason, the question of 'sacramentalism' in John's Gospel is a vital one for us to consider. Let us now turn to consider some key passages which speak of, or allude to, the practice of baptism within John.

1. BAPTISM IN JOHN

The most obvious place to begin our examination of the place that baptism has in John's thought is in connection with the baptism of Jesus by John the Baptist. It seems clear that the subject of baptism was quite a divisive one within the very first years of the Christian movement, if the statement contained in John 3:25–6 is anything to go by. In that couplet we read of a dispute arising out of the relative success of Jesus's baptismal activity in the Jordan river when compared to that of John the Baptist. The dispute is clarified somewhat by the declaration on the lips of John the Baptist, recorded in 1:33, where water baptism and baptism in the Spirit are contrasted. John says in effect: 'God sent me to perform water baptisms, but Jesus will do something even more important; he will baptize you in the Holy Spirit.'

What does all of this mean? On one level discussion about the baptism of John does not necessarily help us very much when it comes to our assessment of sacramentalism since it could be said to belong to an old dispensation, the era of the Old Testament law and prophets, and therefore has nothing to do with Christian baptism. However, such an outright dismissal of John's baptism as having nothing to do with the development of the Christian practice is too harsh. Whatever else we may say, it is indisputable that John's baptism helped influence the Christian practice of baptism in terms of both mode (the fact that it was performed by immersion in water) and at least part of its theological meaning (as a sign of repentance before God). Perhaps the most important conclusion to be drawn at this point is that the ritual water baptism performed by John the Baptist was the main antecedent to Christian baptism as it came to be practised later in the Church.

At the same time, this water baptism of John the Baptist is contrasted with the Spirit baptism associated with Jesus Christ himself, as the Johannine passage just cited demonstrates. There are points of continuity and points of discontinuity between John's baptism and Jesus's. That much seems clear and undisputed. But precisely *how* are the two baptisms related? In what way are they drawn together? Would it be true to say that John's water baptism of repentance finds its fulfilment in the Christian sacrament of baptism? If so, what connection is there between this water baptism and the Spirit baptism performed by Jesus of which the Baptist spoke? To put the question in another form, one dealing more directly with the Christian sacramentalism with which we are concerned, we could ask: How do the physical and the spiritual aspects of Christian baptism interrelate? It is in seeking the answer to these questions that a closer examination of three key passages of John's Gospel is in order. We shall examine 3:3–5; 13:1–17 and 19:34 in turn.

We have already had an opportunity to note briefly the exchange between Jesus and Nicodemus recorded in John 3 earlier in chapters 1 and 6 when we were discussing the idea of the 'kingdom of God' within John. The critical verse for our consideration here is John 3:5: 'Truly, truly, I say to you, unless one is born of water and the Spirit he cannot enter the kingdom of God.' There are basically two interpretations of the reference to 'born of water', one which emphasizes the sacramental significance of the idea and associates it with Christian baptism, and one which downplays the sacramental idea altogether and takes it to be simply a metaphor of physical birth. The fact that both interpretations have been put forward by competent and dedicated Christian scholars from various ecclesiastical traditions should alert us to the exegetical uncertainties the passage contains. What are the strengths of each position? Let us examine both approaches. Having done that, we will then be in a better position to make up our own minds concerning John's teaching about baptism as contained in this discourse with Nicodemus.

Firstly, what are the reasons for taking 'born of water' in John 3:5 as a reference for physical birth and thus disassociating it from the Christian sacrament of baptism altogether? The primary reason this has been suggested is the very next verse, John 3:6: 'That which is born of the flesh is flesh, and that which is born of the Spirit is spirit.' In other words a parallelism is set up in 3:5–6 which might be set out like this:

John 3:5   John 3:6

of water = that which is born of flesh (physical birth)
of Spirit = that which is born of Spirit (spiritual birth)

Those who argue for this interpretation find the illustration of a physical birth of a human being helpful to their case. The fact that human birth is associated with the breaking of the amniotic sac (the 'waters') is thought to strengthen the argument, as does the reference to 'the womb' on Nicodemus's lips in 3:4. To put it simply, the interpretation of John 3:5 is governed by the meaning of John 3:6; one effectively works backwards from the latter verse and interprets the earlier in light of it.

Alternatively, what are the reasons for taking 'born of water' as a reference to the sacrament of Christian baptism? The primary reason for interpreting John 3:5 in this way is the earlier verse of the dialogue, namely 3:3: 'Truly, truly, I say to you, unless one is born from above, he cannot see the kingdom of God.' Here another parallelism can be set up, one which looks like this:

John 3:3		John 3:5
Truly, truly I say to you,	=	Truly, truly I say to you,
unless one is born	=	unless one is born
from above	=	of water and the Spirit
he cannot see	=	he cannot enter
the kingdom of God.	=	the kingdom of God.

Those who argue for a sacramental interpretation of John 3:5 point out that the verse is clearly a restatement of the declaration of 3:3 and that it matches this verse point-for-point both in terms of structure and meaning. Thus, the reference to 'baptism of water' is taken to be very closely connected to 'baptism of Spirit' and corresponds to the idea of 'being born from above' in John 3:3. To put this simply, we could say that the interpretation of John 3:5 is governed by the meaning of John 3:3 and the natural reading of the passage (from 3:3 to 3:5) is maintained. The implication of this interpretation is that 'water baptism' and 'Spirit baptism' are seen as essentially one action, a single entity, which is the equivalent of 'being born from above'. The structure of the parallelism would strongly support such an interpretation.

These, broadly stated, are the two possibilities of interpreting the 'born of water' in John 3:5. Historically, Baptists have tended toward the second of these interpretations, and I must confess that I am quite persuaded by it myself. But Baptists have often been accused by others of reading a 'baptismal theology' into each and every reference to 'water' contained in the New Testament, including this verse in John. Is that what we are in danger of doing here? Are there any other considerations which could help us decide what John is trying to communicate to us through this reference to 'born of water' in John 3:5? One or two other points need to be added to the discussion at this juncture.

The first has to do with the main focus of John's contrast in the dialogue with Nicodemus. What is John the Gospel writer trying to contrast for us? Is it really 'physical birth' versus 'spiritual birth', as the first interpretation discussed above suggests? Are 'water' and 'Spirit' points of contrast, or are they complementary points? If they are points of contrast then one is bound to ask why the discussion of 'Spirit' in 3:7-8 completely leaves aside any reference to the 'water birth' side of the contrast. Indeed, in verse 7 we have Jesus restating the declaration made in 3:3 before going on to fill it out by drawing a contrast between the way that 'Spirit birth' operates and the way that the wind works.[3] It thus becomes very difficult to sustain an argument which concentrates physical birth as the explanation for the inclusion of 'water' in the statement of 3:5, in the face of the flow of the rest of the dialogue with Nicodemus. Indeed, the only other reference which even remotely suggests a 'physical birth' (as opposed to 'water baptism') is, as we mentioned, John 3:4 with its reference to 'the womb' of a mother. But this uterine image might itself just as easily have arisen directly from the birth imagery of 3:3.

Second, we have to note that elsewhere in the New Testament there is a strong association between spiritual re-birth and the physical act of water baptism. This is the normal pattern throughout the Pauline letters and the Acts of the Apostles, with a number of passages speaking of the act of belief and water baptism almost as if they are synonymous events, or at least inter-locking ones. This is the essential point of G.R. Beasley-Murray's treatment of the crucial phrase 'in the name of Christ'. He argues persuasively that according to the New Testament, a believer's being 'sealed with the Spirit' takes place in the actual event of water baptism 'in the name of Christ.'[4] So Christian conversion and initiation are inseparably bonded together. Thus one cannot help but wonder if the reference to 'water' in John 3:5 is indeed a reference, admittedly somewhat veiled, to the Christian sacrament of baptism. On balance, it would seem so.

We turn now to consider the second major passage from John's Gospel which is often seen as an expression of its sacramentalism. In John 13:1-17 we have the account of Jesus's final meal with the disciples, a meal which culminates not in a Passover celebration (as it does in the Synoptic gospels), but in a ritual footwashing. This footwashing has sometimes been taken to be an important supplementary role in John's baptismal theology. Some Baptists have gone even farther than that and have actually incorporated ritual footwashing into their ecclesiastical practice, effectively making it a third ordinance.[5] In this regard they follow the practice of many Brethren churches and build upon the long-established tradition of the Moravians institutionalized by Nicholaus von Zinzendorf in the mid-1700's.

Are we correct in reading a veiled allusion to the sacrament of Christian baptism into the story of Jesus's washing the feet of his disciples? It has to be admitted that the baptismal connection is not immediately obvious, although Peter's response to Jesus's action in verse 9 gets close. Peter states: 'Lord, wash not only my feet, but my hands and my head also!' Still, I find it difficult to accept that a baptismal image is being deliberately invoked by the writer in the passage.

Yet, at the same time, Canon Fenton has rightly remarked that it is entirely fitting that the Synoptic account of the Lord's Supper has become replaced by the story of the footwashing in John in that there is a theme common to both images: 'Both eucharist and foot-washing point to the laying down of life for others, as food, or as a slave.'[6] The issue then becomes whether we feel that this image of humility, of servitude on the part of Christ, necessarily commits us to a sacramental understanding of the story in John 13. It may indeed be doing just that, but only on a secondary level. Surely the main point of the footwashing episode was that it stood as an enactment of what true humility and service means for the disciples, and through them for the believing Church. Baptism as a sacrament may be related to this idea of humility, as it most certainly was and is, but that is not the primary underlying truth being communicated by the practice of baptism in the Church. To put it bluntly, the Church does not practice baptism to demonstrate Christian humility, but conversion and incorporation into the Body of Christ. In short, I find little to commend the idea that John 13 teaches us about the Christian sacrament of baptism.

Third, a further cryptic verse from John's Gospel which is often taken to have sacramental significance is 19:34: 'But one of the soldiers pierced his side with a spear, and at once there came out blood and water.' This incidental detail is not contained within the Synoptic Gospel accounts of the crucifixion. The famous hymn of Augustus Montague Toplady entitled 'Rock of Ages' is based in part on this verse from John's Gospel. In the first verse of that hymn Toplady wrote:

> Rock of Ages, cleft for me,
> Let me hide myself in Thee;
> Let the water and the blood,
> From Thy riven side which flowed,
> Be of sin the double cure;
> Cleanse me from its guilt and power.

Some have argued that by the references to 'water' and 'blood', John is alluding to the sacraments of baptism and Lord's Supper respectively. The dual liquids flowing from the very heart of Christ are quite a striking image, to be sure. In fact, the crucifixion has often been depicted in Christian art with an angel holding a chalice to collect the blood flowing from the wound in Christ's side. This is how, for example, Dürer's woodcut series of 1510–11 entitled 'The Great Passion' portrays the crucifixion scene. No doubt this illustrates the fact that the crucifixion was often later understood in eucharistic terms, but is that what John 19:34 intends? Can we really take the references to 'blood' and 'water' to have been primarily directed to such a sacramental purpose? Two things must be said in response.

First, it is perhaps possible to take the reference to the 'blood' to be a veiled allusion to the Lord's Supper, given what we know elsewhere about the cup of wine and its association with the death of Christ. But the association of the 'water' in 19:34 with the sacrament of baptism can only be arrived at by means of a rather tortuous exegetical route, which is dependent on some very speculative conceptual associations. We could almost say that it is arrived at only because it rides the coat-tails of the sacramental associations of the 'blood/Lord's Supper' idea. Is baptism really the first thing that the readers would have understood by the verse? And if we think that unlikely, do we really have very solid ground for thinking that just such an idea was what the author intended?

Second, assuming for the moment that such an overt sacramentalism is not the intention of 19:34, we might move on to ask, what is? What is John wishing to communicate if not the ideas of baptism and the Lord's Supper here? The simplest answer is that he is wanting to emphasize the reality of Jesus's death. Many scholars feel that John is combating a docetic interpretation of Jesus's death, one which argued that Jesus only *appeared* to die physically and that in reality he was only on earth as a spiritual being. This, they would say, is refuted in a number of places within John's Gospel, notably in his thundering incarnational statement of 1:14. Thus, John 19:34 is best seen as a further testimony to Jesus's real, physical death since spirits do not bleed when stabbed through the heart. But why is it *water* and blood? The answer to this may lie in the fact that human blood very quickly breaks down biologically into constituent parts (serum and blood cells) and this would have the appearance of water and blood. The reference to 'water and blood' thus becomes a medical description of a process known as sero-sanguination. It is worth noting in this regard that John 19:33 makes specific mention of the fact that this spear-stabbing was done after Jesus was already dead, that is to say that the separation of the blood into liquid and cells would have already begun. In short, it is probably best to interpret 19:34 as containing a sacramental declaration only with certain reservations. The thrust of this particular verse lies more with its anti-docetic character, the fact that Jesus's full and unqualified humanity is thereby affirmed.[7]

We now turn to consider the place that the Lord's Supper has in Johannine theology.

2. THE LORD'S SUPPER IN JOHN

We have noted above in connection with John 19:34 the likelihood that a eucharistic inference is contained within the verse. Almost everyone would agree that this is the case. But by far the most important passage for discussing the Lord's Supper in John is found in chapter 6 — the so-called 'Bread of Life' discourse. The initial setting of the story is, of course, the 'sign' of the feeding of the five thousand (6:1–14) on the opposite side of the Sea of Galilee. Following this miracle Jesus withdraws to a place of seclusion (6:15). This is followed by a brief account of Jesus's walking on the Sea of Galilee (6:16–21), a passage which relates how Jesus travels back across the lake and serves to set up the dialogue which will occupy the rest of the chapter. The next day in Capernaum Jesus is approached by the multitude and we have an extended account of his discussions with the people, including the 'I am the bread of life' declaration (6:22–71).

It is within this extended discussion that we have two statements of Jesus which seem to be allusions to the Lord's Supper. For instance, in John 6:51 Jesus says: 'I am the living bread which came down from heaven; if any one eats of this bread he will live forever; and the bread which I shall give for the life of the world is my flesh.' Even more to the point is 6:53–8, with its climactic eucharistic declaration: 'Truly, truly, I say to you, unless you eat the flesh of the Son of man and drink his blood, you have no life in you; he who eats my flesh and drinks my blood has eternal life, and I will raise him up at the last day.' It is universally recognized that this second declaration is the most explicit statement within the Gospel about the sacrament of the Lord's Supper. At the very least we would say that this statement has almost exclusively been interpreted in eucharistic terms, from as early as the patristic period. For example, Augustine, Ambrose, and Cyril of Jerusalem all understood the verse in this way.

But how does the declaration itself arise? It is given in answer to the question of the Jews stated in verse 52: 'How can this man give us his flesh to eat?' Whenever I read that particular verse I remember a remarkably similar question being put to me by an inquisitive Arab merchant while I was on a visit to Egypt. It was a few years ago and my wife and I were visiting my parents-in-law who were working in the Nile delta on an irrigational development project. We were invited to the house of one of the leaders of a village and sat in the shade under a canopy of lemon trees and fruit vines in the blazing late-afternoon sun. When our host discovered in casual conversation that we were Christians he said to me, his brow knit in furrows of deep concentration as he struggled to find the correct phrasing in English: 'Tell me about the Man-Feast. I never understood it. Why do you do that?' I was completely floored and did not really understand what he was asking. What did he mean — the 'Man-Feast'? It was only after several minutes of gently probing conversation that I eventually figured out that he was asking about the meaning of the Christian celebration of the eucharist. Where he had originally received his information about Christian beliefs and practice, I have no idea. Apparently he had taken the references to 'eating and drinking the flesh and blood' literally and wanted to know if the rumours he had heard about Christian cannibalism were true. No doubt the question raised by the Jews in 6:53 similarly arises from the incomprehensibility of Jesus's words about himself as the bread/flesh of the world.

It has been noted by many scholars and students of the Gospel of John that the tone of 6:51–8 is markedly different from that seen elsewhere in the rest of the chapter. That is to say, in 6:51–8 the *explicit* identification of Jesus's own body, his flesh and blood, with the bread of life is made. This difference in tone has led some commentators to suggest that what we have in 6:51–8 is a later interpolation into the earlier bread of life discourse, perhaps by a later editor of the Gospel. Rudolf Bultmann, for instance, is of this opinion when he says: 'the terminology of 6:51b–58 is taken from a quite different circle of ideas from that of 6:27–51a. Thus we must inevitably conclude that vv. 51b–58 have been added by an ecclesiastical editor'.[8] Not all have agreed with this as an answer, however. C.K. Barrett feels that any interpolation theory breaks the essential structure of the discourse as a whole and fails to recognize how integrated the discussion is, flowing quite naturally from 'bread of life' to 'flesh and blood' and back to 'bread of life' again. It is no easy solution to sub-divide the passage in the way that Bultmann suggests. Thus, Barrett remarks:

The fact is... that the discourse must be read and understood as a whole. ...We must go back to the miracle of the five thousand. This was a sign; it contained within itself a valid, if partial, representation of the truth about Jesus, who does bring food where there is hunger and thus — taking the scene to the limit — life where there is death.'

Barrett has raised an important point here, one which flows in part out of our discussion about the place that the 'signs' have within the Gospel of John. It certainly cannot be overlooked that this strongly eucharistic passage of 6:51-8, whatever we may feel about it in terms of its being a later editorial addition or not, is set within the context of the feeding of the five thousand. This must govern our preaching and teaching about it, whatever we decide about the sacramental aspects of the passage. As Gerald Sloyan has cautiously remarked: 'Whoever opts to preach on this chapter needs to stay close to the Johannine intent, which is to make Jesus as the food of the believer the deepest meaning of the multiplication story.'[10] This emphasis on the 'sign' context of the eucharistic discourse leads us to consider one final matter before concluding the chapter.

3. THE SACRAMENTS: MAGICAL ACTS OR EMPTY SYMBOLS?

A number of years ago William Peter Blatty's film *The Exorcist* caused quite a stir in towns and cities around the country. I remember late one evening having my uncle telephone me in a state of blind panic. He had just returned home from seeing the film and was terrified by the whole idea of demon possession. He was desperate to find someone who would baptize his little six-month old daughter that very night before she too became the victim of some evil demon. It became quite clear in talking to him that in his mind there was something magical about the physical act of baptism which would prevent the baby from such possession. He wanted her 'done', 'protected' from evil spirits by the physical act of baptism in water. 'I want her to have some guard against demons, just like people are protected against vampires by garlic', he said to me.

Whatever our view of the relationship between the grace of God and the physical elements of the sacraments, we can all recognise the danger here of reducing them to magical acts, divorcing the physical action from the presence and purpose of a personal God. On the other hand, we need to be careful that we do not go too far in the other extreme and evacuate the sacraments completely of any content of grace or significance. We need to avoid what Eduard Schweizer has called the Protestant danger of 'retreat to the Word.'[11] We are to be like a modern Odysseus sailing between our own Scylla and Charybdis, between the twin perils of a magical sacramentalism and an empty symbolism.

It remains true that there is within both the act of baptism and the celebration of the Lord's Supper something which stretches beyond the limits of our understanding, something unfathomable about them as sacramental activities in the Church. As one of the Catholic characters in David Lodge's novel *How Far Can You Go?* is poignantly made to say about the celebration of the Lord's supper:

When my little girl, she's mentally handicapped, wanted to go to Communion with the rest of the family, I didn't see why not. She's always been very interested in the mass, very reverent. Some busybody, a woman in the parish said, "But does she really understand what it's about? Could she explain?" I said, "Could *you?*"[1 2]

The point, rather humorously made by Lodge, is that none of us can comprehend completely the significance of either baptism or the Lord's Supper. Perhaps we all need to recognize that it is not rational explanation of the sacraments that is desired of us by God, but mere acceptance of the experience of his grace that comes through them. There is thus a sense in which all of us are reduced to the state of wonderment in such 'sacramental' matters. Nevertheless, if we are to talk at all about the meaning of a sacramental act, we have a source of valuable insight in the idea of a 'sign' as John develops it in his Gospel.

But is 'sacrament' the correct term at all? Some may object to it, feeling that it is too 'ritualistic' or even 'magical'. For this reason some have preferred the term 'ordinance' instead of 'sacrament' to describe the normal Church practices of baptism and Lord's Supper. Now, certainly there is always the danger of focusing on the ritual acts themselves and not upon the God of grace to whom they witness. That must be accepted as an ever-present danger of human beings, to fail to see beyond the symbolic action. But does that really get us to the heart of the whole 'sacramental' question? If we mean by 'sacrament' something akin to what John meant by his use of the term 'sign' (see page 79) then we are well on the way to an understanding of both baptism and the Lord's Supper as they are presented in the New Testament. Both 'sacraments' (or 'ordinances', if you prefer that term) are then understood as occasions for *revelatory* acts of God; that is to say that in and through them we encounter the God who manifests himself to us in Christ, and come to a greater understanding of him. They reveal God to us and we experience his grace on a deeper level through them.

This revelatory character of the sacraments challenges us as congregations to consider anew what we mean by our practice of baptism and Lord's Supper. Here we strike at one of the most difficult issues associated with both practices — an individualizing tendency, born out of the spirit of our age. Let us consider this for a moment.

It seems to me that we will always run the risk of misunderstanding the essentially 'sacramental' nature of both baptism and the Lord's Supper as long as we continue to treat them as if they were activities designed for the individual believer. In this regard, those of us who stand in the tradition of practising 'believer's baptism' are perhaps even more guilty of mistreating baptism than the Lord's Supper. How often have we treated a baptismal service merely as the public declaration of an individual's faith response, almost as if to say that the purpose of a church baptism is so that we can publicly see John's or Mary's faith? This element of public confession is certainly present within the baptismal service, and we would not want to belittle it or eradicate it. But is it, or should it be, the central focus that we often make it? Surely the essential point for such a public service is not what John or Mary have done, but *what God has done and continues to do through his grace for his people.* How conscious are we of the service as an opportunity for each one of us to experience God's grace afresh through the baptism? Do we dare see it as something given to enhance our collective experience of God? Once we shift the focus of our attention away from the response of the individual and concentrate instead on the corporate life of the congregation, we are going to be much more attentive to recognizing what God himself does for us. The act of baptism, or the celebration of the Lord's Supper, then becomes a celebration of the graciousness of God, and that is not far from what might be termed a strictly sacramental understanding of the ordinances.

4. FIRST COMMUNION IN SPACE

We conclude this chapter with a true story written by Buzz Aldrin, one of the Apollo 11 astronauts who first went to the moon. It is given here in its entirety as first printed in an issue of *Guideposts Magazine* from 1971.[13] Note the way that the story draws together the Lord's Supper with a further text from John's Gospel (15:5), and highlights the revelatory nature, as well as the ecclesiastical setting, of the sacrament itself.

For several weeks prior to the scheduled lift-off of Apollo 11 back in July, 1969, the pastor of our church, Dean Woodruff, and I had been struggling to find the right symbol for the first lunar landing. We wanted to express our feeling that what man was doing in this mission transcended electronics and computers and rockets.

Dean often speaks at our church, Webster Presbyterian, just outside of Houston, about the many meanings of the communion service. 'One of the principal symbols,' Dean says, 'is that God reveals Himself in the common elements of everyday life.' Traditionally, these elements are bread and wine — common food in Bible days and typical products of man's labor.

One day while I was at Cape Kennedy working with the sophisticated tools of the space effort, it occurred to me that these tools were the typical elements of life today. I wondered if it might be possible to take communion on the moon, symbolizing the thought that God was revealing Himself there too, as man reached out into the universe. For there are many of us in the NASA program who do trust that what we are doing is part of God's plan. I spoke with Dean about the idea as soon as I returned home, and he was enthusiastic.

'I could carry the bread in a plastic packet, the way regular inflight food is wrapped. And the wine also — there would be just enough gravity on the moon for liquid to pour.'

I had a question about what scriptural passage to use. Which reading would best capture what this enterprise meant to us? I thought long about this and came up at last with John 15:5. It seemed to fit perfectly. I wrote the passage down on a slip of paper to be carried aboard *Eagle* along with the communion elements. Dean would read the same passage at the service held back home that same day, which would be Sunday, July 20, the day when Neil Armstrong and I were scheduled to be on the surface of the moon. Then we were launched on our flight from Cape Kennedy. The Saturn 5 rocket gave us a rough ride at first, but the rest of the trip through space was smooth.

On the day of the moon landing, we awoke at 5:30 a.m., Houston time. Neil and I separated from Mike Collins in the command module. Our powered descent was right on schedule, and perfect except for one unforeseeable difficulty. The automatic guidance system would have taken *Eagle* to an area with huge boulders. Neil had to steer *Eagle* to a more suitable terrain. With only seconds' worth of fuel left, we touched down at 3.30 p.m.

Now Neil and I were sitting inside *Eagle,* while Mike circled in lunar orbit, unseen in the black sky above us. In a little while after our scheduled meal period, Neil would give the signal to step down the ladder onto the powdery surface of the moon. Now was the moment for communion. So I unstowed the elements in their flight packets. I put them and the Scripture reading on the little table in front of the abort guidance-system computer.

Then I transmitted a message back to NASA headquarters in Houston. 'Houston, this is *Eagle.* This is the LM pilot speaking. I would like to request a few moments of silence. I would like to invite each person listening in, wherever and whoever they may be, to contemplate for a moment the events of the last few hours and to give thanks in his own individual way.' For me this meant taking communion.

In the radio blackout I opened the little plastic packages which contained bread and wine. I poured the wine into the chalice our church had given me. In the one-sixth gravity of the moon, the wine curled slowly and gracefully up the side of the cup. It was interesting to think that the very first liquid every poured on the moon, and the very first food ever eaten there, were communion elements.

And so, just before I partook of the elements, I read the words which I had chosen to indicate our trust that as man probes into space we are in fact acting in Christ. I sensed especially strongly my unity with our church back home, and with the Church everywhere. I read:

'I am the vine, you are the branches. Whoever remains in me, and I in him, will bear much fruit; for you can do nothing without me.'

NOTES TO CHAPTER 7

1   E. Charpentier, *How to Read the New Testament,* (SCM Press, London, 1981), p. 93.

2   J. Fenton, *Finding the Way through John,* (Mowbrays, Oxford, 1988), p. 28.

3   It must not be forgotten that John is making a play on words here in Greek. The same Greek word (pneuma) is used for 'wind' or 'spirit'.

4   G.R. Beasley-Murray, *Baptism in the New Testament,* (Macmillan, London, 1963), p. 171, with special reference to 2 Cor. 1:22, Eph. 1:13, 4:30.

5   The Duck River (and Kindred) Associations of Baptists located in the southern states of the USA is a good example of such a group.

6   J. Fenton *Finding the Way Through John* (n.2 above), p. 62.

7   For a discussion of whether or not John is confronting Doceticism in his Gospel, see the excellent survey article by D. Moody Smith, 'Johannine Studies', in *The New Testament and Its Modern Interpreters,* edited by Eldon Jay Epp and George W. Macrae, (Fortress Press, Philadelphia, 1989), pp. 271-96.

8   R. Bultmann, *The Gospel of John* (ch.1 n.10 above) p. 219.

9   C.K. Barrett, *Essays on John,* (SCM Press, London, 1982), p. 91.

10   Gerald Sloyan, *John,* (John Knox Press, Atlanta, 1988), p. 73.

11   E. Schweizer, *Luke: A Challenge to Present Theology,* (SPCK, London, 1982), p. 67. Schweizer goes on to comment: 'The sacrament becomes a merely symbolic confirmation of what the Word has proclaimed. In this case, it becomes more and more irrelevant.'

12   D. Lodge, *How Far Can You Go?* (Penguin Books, Middlesex, 1980), p. 237. The emphasis is mine.

13   Re-printed by permission of Guideposts Magazine, 757 3rd. Avenue, New York.

QUESTIONS FOR THOUGHT AND DISCUSSION

1.   Eduard Schweizer, *Luke: A Challenge to Present Theology* (ch.7, n.11 above) p. 67, describes the scandal of a common Protestant eucharistic practice which 'if it is celebrated at all on... Sunday, becomes a negligible appendage at the end of the central service of the Word, after which a large part of the congregation has left the church. It is not the Protestant doctrine of the Lord's Supper but the practice which is so alarming.' What does our eucharistic practice reveal about our eucharistic doctrine?

2.   Use a concordance to look up all the references to 'water' in the Gospel of John. How often is it used as a symbol for the earthly, transitory things of life and how often as a symbol for the eternal things of the spirit?

3.   How could we re-structure the normal pattern of our Sunday services to give a greater attention to the significance of the Lord's Supper? What positive benefits have you experienced in making such alterations?

4.   Organize a group within your church to design and create two banners, one to be displayed in baptismal services and one whenever you celebrate the Lord's Supper. Ask them to concentrate on using John 3:5 and 6:53 as the scriptural bases for the designs.

5.   Invite a minister who holds a different theology of baptism from your own to address a small group, and to explain his understanding of baptism. What do you see as the strengths and weaknesses of this position? What steps can be taken within an ecumenical context to maintain the traditional approach of your own church family without appearing to be deliberately confrontational?

VIII

The 'I Am' Sayings

One of the most memorable events associated with John F. Kennedy during his Presidency of the United States was his famous speech delivered in Berlin on June 26, 1963. Kennedy was visiting Berlin at the height of the Cold War between the USA and the USSR, recalling the time when, a few years previously in 1948, a strict blockade on trade and travel into and out of the city had been imposed by Soviet-led forces.[1] It was another tense political situation that had now brought the American President to Berlin, to make his speech before the Berlin Rathaus in Rudolph-Wilde-Platz. In the speech he uttered one of his most famous comments, one which perhaps more than almost any other, has been fixed in our memories of him ever since.

Since he wanted spontaneously to strike a chord of understanding with the Berlin people by saying something to them in German, he took it upon himself to add, as a climax to the speech, 'Ich bin ein Berliner.' What he meant by this, of course, was that he identified with the people of West Berlin, that he shared with them in the struggles of the time.

While on that occasion the crowd listening to him erupted into spontaneous applause, I have been told since by a friend of a later generation who lives in Berlin that he and some of his contemporaries read a quite different meaning into the phrase. While appreciating Kennedy's intention to express his concern about the political situation, many found it incongruous that a stranger should claim such intimate acquaintance with their city and they have exploited for its humorous effect another equally possible meaning for the claim he made. A 'Berliner' is also the name for a special type of pastry filled with sweet preserves, which leaves Kennedy's statement to be something akin to 'I am a jam doughnut'. The temptation to make this reinterpretation is the greater because it is rather unusual in German to speak of being 'a' (ein) Berliner. Thus even such a solemn and noble declaration can be turned by an imaginative mind into something absurd. Kennedy's declaration surely must rank as one of the most memorable 'I am' sayings of our time.

In this chapter of our study of John we come to consider another characteristic feature of the Gospel, namely the 'I am' declarations of Jesus. Just as the people of Berlin have to be perceptive about what Kennedy meant in his famous 'I am' speech, so too, we must be careful that we understand exactly what John was intending to say in the 'I am' statements recorded as on the lips of the Lord Jesus Christ. Some of them may even sound as out of place and cryptic to the listener as Kennedy's speech may now sound to some in Berlin. For instance, can you imagine what the first reaction must have been to 'I am the bread of life'? We must not only hear the words of such 'I am' declarations themselves, but attempt an interpretation of their meaning. That necessary process of interpretation can be a very risky business, one which exposes our own presuppositions and challenges us in our faith. Let us now turn to the 'I am' sayings of Jesus as recorded in John's Gospel.

1. 'EGO EIMI' SAYINGS

The Greek phrase 'egō eimi' ('I am') as applied to Jesus occurs 25 times within the Gospel of John (4:26; 6:20; 6:35, 41, 48, 51; 8:12, 18, 23 (twice), 24, 28, 58; 10:7, 9, 11, 14; 11:25; 13:19; 14:6; 15:1; 15:5; 18:5, 6, 8).[2] Many of the best-known declarations of Jesus about himself are found here. These 'I am' sayings can be divided into four basic groups depending on the type of grammatical declaration made. The first group, perhaps the most recognizable, could be called 'definitive declarations', meaning that Jesus figuratively described himself as 'the...' something or other, such as the door, the bread, the vine. There are seven 'I am' sayings in John which fall into this category:

1. 'I am the bread of life' (6:35, 41, 48).[3]
2. 'I am the light of the world' (8:12).
3. 'I am the door of the sheep' (10:7, 9).
4. 'I am the good shepherd' (10:11, 14).
5. 'I am the resurrection and the life' (11:25).
6. 'I am the way and the truth and the life' (14:6).
7. 'I am the vine (or true vine)' (15:1, 5).

It has often been pointed out that these seven predicate statements involving 'I am' are tied to the extended narrative discourses within the Gospel, and actually function as 'capstones', as summary statements of the discourses themselves. At the same time, several of these 'I am' declarations are quite clearly linked to one of the seven 'signs' of the Gospel. Thus, the statement 'I am the bread of life' summarizes the extended discourse found in 6:22-59 and follows the 'sign' of the feeding of the five thousand in 6:1-15. Similarly, the declaration 'I am the light of the world' is perhaps best taken as a proleptic summary statement on the nature of sight and finds its rather ironic anchor in the 'sign' of the healing of the blind man in chapter 9. Chapter 9 closes with a paragraph on the nature of spiritual blindness, which hearkens back to the 'I am' declaration about light in 8:12, an interpretation strengthened when we recall the statements about the Logos being the light which has come into the world in 1:5, 9. A third example is the declaration 'I am the resurrection and the life', which stands as a summary statement of the extended Lazarus episode in chapter 11, John's penultimate 'sign'.

Ernest Best has rightly pointed out that these 'I am' sayings are closely related to the overall presentation of Jesus as the Revealer in the Gospel of John. Best says that

Jesus is primarily a Revealer and that we 'can see this in the new range of predicates which are applied to him: he is the light of the world, the truth, the way, the Logos. It is seen even more in the long discourses of the Gospel. Their purpose is no longer to instruct men in what it means to love one's neighbour, as is the case in so much of the teaching in Matthew and Luke, but to disclose Jesus' nature and through that to disclose the nature of God'.[4] For the most part, discussions about the 'I am' sayings of John's Gospel have concentrated on these seven instances and it is easy to see why this is so since they are extraordinarily bold declarations by and about Jesus Christ.

These seven figurative statements have also been the subject of some of the most famous artistic representations of Christendom with painters returning to them again and again for inspiration. We note, for instance, Holman Hunt's well-known painting *Christ the Light of the World,* now hanging in the chapel of Keble College, Oxford, or Gerrit van Honthorst's *Christ before the High Priest* in the National Gallery of London, which is reproduced on the cover of this book. A more Johannine painting than Honthorst's it is difficult to imagine since he portrays a Christ in total control, although standing passively before the seated Jewish High Priest. A single, lighted candle between them is the focus of the painting and stands as a powerful illustration of John 8:12. You can almost feel the dark, shadowy background of the painting, perhaps representing the lost world which stands in sharp contrast to the light at the centre of the painting, the Light of Christ. The seven figurative 'I am' sayings have certainly had an extraordinary influence in art and we cannot doubt their importance as Johannine focal texts.

However, in some ways the other 'egō eimi' declarations are even more revealing for us since they may open up new and unusual avenues of understanding the significance of Jesus Christ in John's Gospel. Partly because they are so overshadowed by the better known 'I am' declarations, they are often missed.

A second group of 'egō eimi' sayings uses the 'I am' form followed by a present active participle, functioning as a predicate of the statement. The effect of this construction is to throw emphasis on the *activity* of Jesus in the declaration. There are two such 'I am' declarations in this category.

8. 'I am he who speaks to you' (4:26)
9. 'I am he who bears witness' (8:18)

A third group, slightly more difficult to describe, uses the 'I am' saying as a way for Jesus to make some qualifying statement about himself, though not in a strictly predicative sense. There are three such 'I am' sayings in this category.

10. 'It is I, do not be afraid' (6:20).
11. 'I am from above' (8:23a).
12. 'I am not of this world' (8:23b).

The final group is even more difficult to describe than the last two in that the 'I am' saying is constructed in such a way that it begs the question about the (implied)

predicate of the statement. At times one has to go backward into the context of the
passage to decide this. Many translations supply the word 'he' in order to make sense
of the meaning of the declaration. There are four, or possibly five, such 'I am' sayings
which fall into this category.

13. 'I am (he)' (8:24).
14. 'I am (he)' (8:28)
15. 'I am (he)' (13:19)
16. 'I am (he)' (18:5, 6, 8).
17. 'I am' (8:58).

In some ways the final saying, that contained in 8:58, is the most unusual of all of
the 'I am' declarations because of its far-reaching christological implications. We shall
turn now to consider this particular statement in more detail and use it to explore
more fully some of the christological depth contained within the Gospel of John.

2. THE GREAT 'I AM' OF JOHN 8:58

In John 8:48-59 we have an extended paragraph describing Jesus's clash with the
Jewish leaders over the nature of his authority and his relationship to the patriarch
Abraham. The paragraph moves to the stunning declaration of 8:58: 'Truly, truly,
I say to you, before Abraham was, I am.' Raymond Brown remarks on this verse:
'No clearer implication of divinity is found in the Gospel tradition'.[5] Thus, one of
the most enduring popular interpretations of this declaration is to see it as an allusion
to the statement made by God to Moses in Exodus 3:14. In other words, the 'I am'
declaration becomes an open profession of deity on the lips of Jesus, and the whole
point of the dialogue in John 8:48-58 is that Jesus is thereby revealed to be God
himself. We might even term this interpretation the 'traditional' or 'orthodox' one,
in view of its long history within the Church.

If we focus for a moment on the vigorous reaction by the Jewish leaders to Jesus's
statement, as recorded in 8:59, we might easily think that this is precisely what angered
them. This means that they saw in Jesus's 'I am' declaration an encroachment upon
the sacred ground of Jewish monotheism and that they sought to stone him for
blasphemy as a result. Thus, we have a parallel to the statement made in John 5:18
about Jesus's alleged claim to have God as his Father and thereby 'make himself equal
with God'. What are the grounds for arguing such an interpretation of John 8:58,
one which forges such close links with Exodus 3:14?

G.R. Beasley-Murray notes[6] that the Septuagint (Greek) version of Psalm 89:1-2 is
often included in discussion at this point, with its reported declaration by Moses about
God providing a remarkable parallel to the statement in John 8:58. Psalm 89:1-2 reads:
'Lord, You have been our dwelling place in all generations. Before the mountains
were brought forth, or ever You formed the earth and the world, from everlasting
to everlasting, You are! ('su ei')'. A second passage from the Septuagint, even more

relevant to the point, is Isaiah 43:10-11 which has the Lord God declaring that "'You are my witnesses," says the Lord, "and my servant whom I have chosen, that you may know and believe me and understand that I am ('egō eimi') He. Before me no god was formed, nor shall there be any after me. I, I am the Lord, and besides me there is no saviour'''. This exalted, and unequivocable language is also repeated elsewhere in this same chapter of Isaiah, notably in 43:13, 15, 25. Thus, it is without doubt that the Old Testament contains numerous instances where the eternal presence of God himself is described in terms which are very similar to the 'I am' declaration of John 8:58. But should such instances be taken as evidence that the Johannine passage is making a declaration about the complete union of the *being* of Jesus with the *being* of God? To ask the question once again: Does John intend for us to understand by this statement that Jesus is claiming to be the great 'I am', Yahweh Himself? Is what is being proclaimed in John 8:58 Jesus's full deity? Is this a New Testament declaration that Jesus is the second person of the Trinity? These are difficult questions to answer, but central ones to consider if we wish to understand the christological message of the Gospel of John.

Given what we know about other passages in John, passages which are extremely significant christologically, it appears that such 'ontological' identification (ie an identity of 'being') between Jesus and God is to take the meaning of the declaration of John 8:58 a step too far. I should make clear that while I shall be wanting to affirm a little later the divinity of Jesus in his very being, here I am simply concerned with the meaning of *this* text as the evangelist wrote it. Certainly Jesus is wanting to contrast his own existence with that of Abraham; that is clearly the point of the statement as a whole. That is why there is a deliberate change of Greek verb tenses within the statement: 'Before Abraham *came to be, I am.*' (an aorist verb followed by one in the present tense). The point is exactly the same one made through the change in verb tenses in John 1:1-4, 14. There the Logos exists before the creation, whenever we wish to place it and however far back in the mists of time we wish to conceive it. It is not to be understood as a statement about chronology alone, but as a deliberate declaration of contrast between the pre-existent Word and the historical figure Abraham. Or, to put it another way, John 8:58 is a contrast between Abraham's historical or chronological entrance into existence and Jesus Christ's timeless existence.

Even if we were to accept that in 8:58 Jesus (or John) is deliberately wishing to emphasize the Old Testament 'I am' declarations which have God as their subject, and apply them to himself (or Jesus) we may be in danger of missing the essential point of the passage. Many scholars have advised caution on this point, wisely suggesting that we proceed carefully. Rudolf Schnackenburg, for instance, is quite supportive of the idea that we have in John 8:58 a deliberate allusion to Exodus 3:14, yet emphasizes that the Old Testament focus is not upon the abstract, metaphysical nature of God, but upon his steadfastness and faithful desire to redeem his people. On this basis Schnackenburg continues: 'In the same way Jesus's adoption of the divine saying contains an appeal to them to listen to him as the one in whom the God of their fathers, the God of Abraham, Isaac and Jacob, has come to them to fulfil his saving purposes.'[7] In a very real sense then, to focus attention on Jesus within this passage, and to concentrate on his own divine identity, is to miss the essential point. This is so because throughout John's Gospel Jesus's identity is wholly derived from his mission, his task, which is to do the Father's work and accomplish the redemption of the world. He is identified with his Father in his *activity*.

If, as I have been suggesting, the main point of the declaration in John 8:58 is misconceived if it is approached from the standpoint of its being a declaration of Jesus's divine being, what are we to make of John 8:59? Why do the Jewish leaders pick up stones and seek to kill Jesus? Is it not because he is blaspheming God by declaring himself to be God's equal? Surely, so the argument goes, it is precisely because they felt that Jesus had gone too far and made himself equal to God, and therefore deserved the capital punishment for blasphemy, a violent death by stoning. This has always been one of the most powerful secondary reasons for interpreting the 'I am' declaration in 8:58 as an allusion to the 'I am' of Exodus 3:14. But how reliable is this suggestion? Here two other key passages from John come into the discussion. This question of Jesus's relationship to God is precisely what lies at the heart of both 5:18 (alluded to above) and 10:18–19. Yet, it is important to note that all three instances (5:18; 10:18–19 and 8:58–9) describe a debate amongst the Jewish leaders which focuses on the meaning of Jesus's actions, the fact that he described his earthly task as doing the Father's work. Thus it appears that we may be misunderstanding the essential point of debate by focusing exclusively on Jesus's divine identity as the 'sticking point' in the Jewish leaders' minds. A further point needs to be raised in this regard.

Surely we must also admit the possibility that it is not so much a comparison between Jesus and God that raises the temperatures of the Jewish leaders, but the fact that the great patriarchal figure Abraham has been humiliated by Jesus's statement. In other words, it is entirely possible to say that the threatened stoning arises out of Jesus's challenge to the position and honour of Abraham, and not because Jesus was seen to be challenging the identity of God himself. This seems to be the natural inference of the passage as a whole with 8:53 voicing the Jewish leaders' protest in precisely these terms. In addition, the figure of Abraham appears earlier in the chapter in 8:33–40 where the Jewish leaders and Jesus carry on a debate about the meaning of true sonship, which again emphasizes the deeds of a true follower of God.

Is this not the essential point of that other classic Johannine text which causes us so much difficulty, 10:30, yet another declaration which causes the Jewish leaders to pick up stones in order to kill Jesus? In 10:30 Jesus declares: 'I and the Father are one.' But we should ask: 'One' in what sense? Is it to be understood as a declaration that Jesus *is* simply God himself, that he is Yahweh, the Great 'I Am' (and thus a close parallel to 8:58)? A closer reading of the passage will surely confirm that the context of the declaration in 10:30 is a unity of purpose between Jesus and God, the fact that Jesus is *doing* the works of his Father and that they are united in the desire to bring about the great work of salvation for humankind. In short, we should be very careful that we do not read too much into Jesus's statement in 10:30, especially when we also have other declarations such as 14:28: 'The Father is greater than I'. They are easily understood as compatible if taken as declarations about the redemptive activity of God in Christ. To put it another way, John's purpose here is not to make a christological point on the purely ontological level (ie a union of being), but on a functional one (ie a union of doing). I shall have more to say about this distinction as our discussion proceeds, but meanwhile we should listen to Edward Schillebeeckx on this point:

John puts forward a functional christology, but not in the modern sense of this word. John's preference for verbs over nouns is very striking. He sees the relationship between Jesus and God in functional terms, as emerges clearly from the arguments put forward by the Johannine Jesus (10:34–38). For John, Jesus is really man, but in a unique, all-surpassing relationship with God. Anyone who knows him, knows the Father (8:19), and anyone who sees him sees the Father (14:9). What Jesus says and does reveals his person, that is the mystery of his life with the Father. In this sense the function is his person itself.[8]

In light of this perceptive comment, let us return to 8:58 for a moment.

Given the natural link between the declaration that Jesus is before Abraham and the discussion about what it means to be a child of God (and of Abraham!), it is quite easy to see how the 'traditional' interpretation of John 8:58 later arises. However, we must be careful not to allow the hypothetical possibilities of interpretation to be construed as absolute certainties in this matter. I, for one, am open to the possibility of an interpretation which sees the 'I am' declaration in 8:58 as a deliberate allusion (by Jesus or John) to Exodus 3:14, and thus an absolute assertion of Jesus's ontological identification with God. But at the same time I would hasten to add that I am not persuaded that it is something that is necessarily demanded by the text. In fact, I would go so far as to say that it is not the most natural way of understanding this verse. Nor do I see it as necessarily dishonouring to take the main point of the declaration to be one involving Jesus's timelessness (his pre-existence before Abraham) rather than his deity. This leads us to one further consideration.

3. THE IDEA OF PRE-EXISTENCE IN JOHN

Before concluding our discussion it is necessary to explore one final, but crucial, theological area. We need to grasp what lies at the centre of John's christological message about the pre-existence of Jesus Christ. This can be best done in the form of a question: what sort of relationship is there between the concept of the pre-existence of Jesus, and a statement about his deity? The former we can find expressed in a number of places in the New Testament, including John; but the latter is not present *in the form* with which we are now familiar, the classic statements that were worked out later in the Church and which came to full expression in the creeds of Nicaea (CE 325) and Chalcedon (CE 451). One of our methodological difficulties when it comes to interpreting the New Testament documents is that we live after Nicaea and Chalcedon, and the traditional language about the trinitarian relationship between Jesus Christ the Son and God the Father is very much part of our Christian inheritance. It is very difficult for us to resist anachronistically reading back those formulations into the New Testament documents, though I shall be explaining how the foundations for them are certainly there.

John has very carefully formulated his thoughts on these matters, and we would do well to pay close attention to what he does say and what he does not. I suggest this is a very important matter simply because of John's own Jewish setting and background. Thus, it is crucial if we wish to see how John has worked within the bounds of Jewish thought, how he has built upon the conventions of his own day and yet, in the light of the Christ-event, moved adventurously beyond them. Let us explore this for a moment.

In the first place we need to recognize that in John's thought-world it was entirely possible for someone to believe in the pre-existence of an attribute of God, such as Wisdom. This meant that the fullness of deity could be ascribed to this attribute, yet without exhausting God in the process of doing so. Wisdom, for instance, might be said to be pre-existent, existing in the mind of God before time began (as it is said to do in *Wisdom of Solomon*[7]). 'Wisdom' was certainly understood as being *from* God, it was clearly an attribute *of* God himself, and was in that sense *identified* with God. But 'wisdom' as an idea could never be said to empty or exhaust the being of God.

Having said that, we need at the same time to go on and say that all of the Jewish and Hellenistic parallels to pre-existence, such as wisdom and Torah (the Law), are simply pre-existent *ideas*. That is to say, they are expressions of divine concepts, or personifications of attributes of God. Many of these are known and recognized as being an important part of the Jewish thought-world of the first century, particularly within the Hellenistic world of someone like Philo of Alexandria. But the critical question is what happens when these notions of pre-existence begin to move beyond this purely conceptual level and become applied to a specific historical figure, namely Jesus of Nazareth. Does this not mean that a new dynamic has been interjected, that things have begun to head in a new direction? It almost certainly does, and this is surely one of the most important reasons why an ever-widening divide between Jews and Christians first appeared and quickly developed after Jesus's resurrection. What we now describe as 'the Christian movement' may have begun within the bounds of an enlightened Second Temple Judaism, but it could not stay there for very long.

The application of these ideas of pre-existence to a human being, and one known to have recently lived, died and been resurrected, is an astonishing theological development. We are not going too far to say that it was an unprecedented event within first-century Judaism. As G.B. Caird once remarked:

Jewish antecedents adequately explain all the terminology used in the New Testament to describe the pre-existent Christ, but they cannot explain how Christians came to belief in his pre-existence as a person; for the Jews had believed only in the pre-existence of a personification. Wisdom was a personification, either of a divine attribute or of a divine purpose, but never a person.[9]

When we come to identify a divine attribute, such as wisdom, with a human being, there is a significant distinction to be made. There is a difference between saying that someone '*has* the wisdom of God' and saying that someone '*is* the wisdom of

God'. This is a difference which is sometimes described in terms of a shift from a 'functional' to an 'ontological' understanding. To say that someone *has* the wisdom of God means that through that person's activities we detect the hand of God in operation, that we see God working through his agent. On the other hand, to say that someone *is* the wisdom of God is to take an additional theological step and invest that person with the very being of God himself. Here the relationship has moved beyond a matter of agency to that of a matter of *being* (ontology).

Now, it is abundantly clear that sections of Judaism were quite happy with a 'functional' understanding of someone as embodying divine wisdom, but resisted an 'ontological' identification of someone with God. In early Christian thought, the association of Jesus with an attribute of God, like wisdom, stood in the first place as a declaration of God's working in and through the person of Jesus of Nazareth. It is a statement of a functional christology or, as some have expressed it, a 'christology from below'. But we must observe that such was the impact of Jesus upon his followers, that there was an inevitable movement from a functional understanding of his person to an ontological one. I believe that this was a proper response, that the purely functional assessment of him as one who stands as God's agent in the working out of the divine purposes is, in the final analysis, insufficient. Jesus Christ is not only God's agent in the field, as it were, but God himself living and working in the world. This is an ontological christology or, as some have expressed it, a 'christology from above'.

The two approaches, from below and above, should not in my opinion be seen as contradictory; both are needed to begin to express the wonder of God in Jesus Christ, accomplishing the redemption of the world. When we turn to the New Testament texts themselves, however, it is sometimes exceedingly difficult to know if what is being expressed in a given passage proceeds on a functional basis of christology, or whether it has actually moved beyond that to the ontological level. In the main, the New Testament is more clearly functional in its christological message. Only rarely do we see an ontological christology expressed. If we are, then, always seeking to find an ontological expression of Jesus's deity in the scriptures, we may be pressing the fragile documents to the breaking point. If we are not careful, we may fail to appreciate the delicately poised way in which these matters are presented. We may seek to extract from the New Testament a christological exactness and precision of expression which is not there, and we may miss the actual insights that *are* there for us.

Let us return to the Prologue of John's gospel to highlight the key matter. It is important to see that John very carefully and delicately makes his christological point here. He avoids ever saying that the man, Jesus of Nazareth, was pre-existent; in the Prologue it is the *Logos* which is explicitly said to be in the beginning with God, not Jesus. True, it is the man Jesus of Nazareth that the Logos becomes, but the movement is in this direction — from pre-existent Logos to man. In other words, and this is the wonder of what John accomplishes here in the Prologue, there is an incarnational thrust in the passage. It leads our thought from divine agency to divine being.

At the same time, this truth of the incarnation of God in the person of Jesus Christ causes us to think again, in many profound ways, about the very being of God himself. Through the incarnation of the Logos, God is thereby revealed to us in a new way, and our comprehension of him can never be what it was before. John's proclamation that the pre-existent Logos has become identified with the person of Jesus of Nazareth is bound then to say something significant about Jesus's relationship to God himself. It leads inevitably and inexorably to the connection between pre-existence and deity.

This assertion, along with the interpretation of the death of Jesus as the atoning action of God, becomes the christological scandal which ultimately meant that Christianity could not co-exist with Judaism, that a 'parting of the ways' was inevitable. This is the 'scandal' of christology which lies at the heart of our faith. Once the pre-existent Logos becomes inextricably identified with the person of Jesus of Nazareth, the stage is set for a christological revolution to occur. The seeds are sown for a daring experiment in christology which eventually comes to flower centuries later in the form of the Nicene and Chalcedonian creeds. We can say that the Christian doctrine of the Trinity was the inevitable, even the necessary, outcome of this daring christological experiment which John helps to initiate and to which he gives expression.

Finally, as we have been examining the 'I am' sayings in some depth, it is appropriate to close with a brief prayer recalling Jesus's declaration in 8:12. It also challenges us to our task of following the example of our Lord Jesus and shining as beacons of light in this world.[10]

Holy Father, at the beginning you said, 'let there be light'
  and there was light.
Yours is the light of every day since then:
  we praise you.

Holy Son, you are the light of the world;
no follower of yours will walk in darkness
but will have the light of life:
  we praise you.

Holy Spirit, you came to the first disciples
with power like tongues of fire.
Yours is the courage that supports us now:
  we praise you.

Father, Son and Holy Spirit, One God to endless ages,
  Renew your light in our hearts,
  Scatter the shadows of evil
  and kindle your flame of love among us. Amen.

NOTES TO CHAPTER 8

1   Quite coincidentally, the day after I finished writing this chapter we witnessed the tearing

down of the Berlin wall, the symbol of the Cold War for nearly 30 years. Time will tell what changes this important symbolic event foretells in East–West relations, but I cannot help but find my thoughts wandering to Ephesians 2:14. The destruction of this wall is perhaps the nearest modern equivalent to the Jewish/Gentile barrier of which that epistle speaks.

2   The phrase in 14:3 should not be included in the discussion here since it clearly implies location and does not stand as a description of Jesus himself or of his activities. It is best translated 'where I am (located)'.

3   6:51 gives us the variation 'I am the living bread'.

4   Ernest Best, *From Text to Sermon: Responsible Use of the New Testament in Preaching,* 2nd edition (T & T Clark, Edinburgh, 1988), p. 25.

5   Raymond Brown, *The Gospel According to John,* Volume 1 (ch.3 n.1 above) p. 367.

6   G.R. Beasley-Murray, *John* (ch.3 n.5 above) pp. 139-140.

7   R. Schnackenburg, *The Gospel According to St. John,* Volume 2, transl. C. Hastings et. al. 1980 (ch.6 n.5 above) p. 224.

8   E. Schillebeeckx, *Christ: The Christian Experience in the Modern World,* (SCM Press, London, 1980), p. 431.

9   G.B. Caird, 'The Development of the Doctrine of Christ in the New Testament', in *Christ for Us Today,* edited by Norman Pittenger, (SCM Press, London, 1968), p. 79.

10   The prayer was written by Paul Fiddes and is contained within the servicebook entitled *Regent's Park College: Prayers and Orders for Worship,* first printed in 1989.

QUESTIONS FOR THOUGHT AND DISCUSSION

1.   Prepare a study series on the 'Seven 'I Am' Sayings of Jesus' which attempts to compare and contrast Old Testament imagery with the New Testament declarations. Use the following pairings for your study comparisons:

     1.   John 6:35 with Exodus 16:13–31
     2.   John 8:12 with Isaiah 60:1–5
     3.   John 10:7, 9 with Ezekiel 34
     4.   John 10:11 with Psalm 23
     5.   John 11:25 with Daniel 12:1–4
     6.   John 14:6 with Proverbs 4:1–19
     7.   John 15:1, 5 with Psalm 80:8–18

2.   Read through the Psalms and compile a list of ways in which the Lord God is described in terms of titles. How does this inform our understanding of his role as the Redeemer?

3. D. Moody Smith, *John* (ch.6 n.4 above) p. 92, remarks on John 8:58: 'Jesus' priority in time points to his priority in being, in relationship to God, in the purpose of God, in significance for humanity.' What do you think he means by this? Is it a helpful description of the verse?

4. We often talk of Jesus Christ's pre-existence, but how correct is it to say that we should also note his 'post-existence' within the New Testament documents? In what ways is Jesus Christ 'post-existent'? Is it an oversimplification to say that Jesus Christ's pre-existent role is that of agent in creation while his post-existent one is that of agent in judgement?

5. Examine a reproduction of Holman Hunt's *Christ as the Light of the World,* or Honthorst's *Christ Before the High Priest* (reproduced on the cover of this book). In what ways do they challenge us to a fresh examination of the meaning of John 8:12?

6. In a small group setting provide each member with a copy of a recent current-affairs magazine or journal (Newsweek, The Economist, or such like), a piece of card, glue and scissors. Ask them to compose a montage of contemporary images which challenge us to consider ways in which Jesus Christ comes to our world saying 'I am...'. One might, for instance, wish to construct a picture of Christ as saying 'I am the Healer of illness' and use various medical-based photographs, including people suffering with AIDS. Discuss which images are important for our times and why.

IX

The Johannine 'Himalayas'

The following question was once set in a Music final examination paper: 'Mark Twain said, "Wagner's music looks better than it sounds; Puccini's sounds better than it looks". Discuss'. As we laugh, our own musical tastes may also be revealed, depending on how loudly we chuckle, and at which half of the quip. The fact is that in this area of life, as in so many others, truth is not what it first seems, reality being more complex than initial observations might immediately suggest. First appearances and initial impressions of the written works of both Puccini and Wagner can be enormously misleading; full appreciation requires our hearing the work performed. And, as we have hinted, our reactions may reveal far more about us than they do about the music or the composers themselves.

The same truth about first impressions holds within the theological realm, particularly when we are dealing with the weightier matters of Christian faith and belief. Things are often not as they first appear. Nowhere is this more true within the Gospel of John than in his use of the title 'Son of God'. The role that a 'Son of God' christology has in the Gospel is of paramount importance, some would even say it is the key declaration of the body of the Gospel, standing alongside the Logos doctrine of the Prologue in John 1:1–18 as the crowning glories of the work. We might even describe the Johannine concepts of 'Son of God' and 'Word' as the 'Himalayas of New Testament christology'. But it is also fair to say that John's 'Son of God' concept is one of the most difficult in the whole of the New Testament to understand. To repeat, things are not always as they first appear.

As a simple illustration of this, may I relate the problems that the title 'Son of God' once presented to our college chapel service programme? A couple of years ago we had as our termly theme 'The Titles of Christ in the Gospels'. As New Testament tutor I was asked to draw up a list of six titles, along with suitable texts, to serve as the basis for our weekly exposition. I chose to approach the task by moving from titles which focused on Jesus's earthly life to those which spoke, increasingly, of his relationship to God, progressing from a 'low' christology to a 'high' one. Thus, we had in the first week of chapel the title 'The Teacher'; in the second, 'The Lord'; in the third, 'The Prophet', and so on. The final week of term was given over to 'The Word' in recognition of the soaring theological statement made in the Prologue of John. But what about the titles 'The Son of Man' and 'The Son of God'? Where were they to be placed in the scheme of things? On the basis of the New Testament meanings of the terms I placed 'Son of God' before 'Son of Man' and submitted the list to the chapel committee responsible for this matter. However, I discovered a few days later that when the list was distributed, the place that the two titles had in the scheme had been reversed, that 'Son of God' was after 'Son of Man' and therefore next to 'The Word' as a statement of quite an exalted christological expression. A colleague admitted to me that he had been responsible for the transposition and we had an interesting and stimulating discussion about it.

Who was right? And why? In fact, both of us were right, depending on which starting point we adopted, depending on which presuppositions we operated with. It is generally accepted that from a New Testament perspective the title 'Son of God' does indeed stand 'lower' on the scale of christological expression than does 'Son of Man'. So, from the strictly biblical point of view, I was right. However, from the standpoint of Church history and doctrinal development, 'Son of God' is the more exalted of the two terms. Thus, from the systematic theologian's point of view, my colleague was correct. The matter highlights one of the difficulties facing us when we consider New Testament christology, particularly those declarations contained within the Gospel of John.

John's idea of the 'Son of God' presents us with a complex problem, one filled with a host of attendent theological and historical considerations. In this regard it presents problems which the Johannine 'Logos' declaration does not, because the 'Word' has not undergone the same sort of theological shift in meaning. The meaning and significance of 'Logos' has certainly been expanded and expounded in the course of theological reflection over the centuries, but it has not had to break free from its biblical 'moorings', so to speak, in the way that 'Son of God' has.

Why then is the christological title 'Son of God' so problematic for us? Several important factors help to make this so, and we shall examine some of them more fully below. For now, we simply note that we are involved in trying to see John's christological message in its own historical and theological context. At the same time this means we are also needing to recognize our own contemporary setting and its influences upon us.

1. JOHANNINE CHRISTOLOGY IN LIGHT OF THE CHURCH CREEDS

Robin Scroggs begins his recent discussion of Johannine christology with the following words:

High Christology! Jesus Christ is completely divine, is God. This is the judgment universally held of the thought of the Gospel of John. For some people, this is a delightful affirmation. At last we are on the plane of Nicaea. For others, it marks a dark, fateful turn in the road. From now on the genuine humanity of Jesus will become increasingly doubtful and useless. In a sense both perceptions are correct, if one is looking back on the Gospel from later centuries. To understand the Gospel itself, however, it is imperative to avoid such retrospective glances.[1]

Thus Scroggs highlights the fact that one of the main reasons why John's christology, notably concerning the 'Son', is so difficult for us is because of our own inherited theological traditions. When we turn to consider 'Son of God' as a theological concept we are immediately caught in the web of Christian tradition and theological development revolving around the title. The idea of 'Son of God' has long been equated with the idea of 'God the Son' and this colours our vision of the issue. As I hinted in the last chapter when we were discussing John 8:58, the Trinitarian inheritance of the Nicene and Chalcedonian creeds is very strong and continues to exert an enormous influence upon us. Sometimes we are conscious of this influence and sometimes we may not be. More often than not it is simply assumed, accepted without question, as if it has become part of the theological 'furniture' of the Church. Such is the power of an abiding tradition.

Let us be clear about what I mean. I am not saying that the great doctrines of the historic Christian faith, such as the divinity of the 'Son of God', should be in any way denigrated or neglected. Far from it! But we have to recognize that the meaning of 'Son of God' (in particular) is a product of generations of subsequent development and reflection upon the biblical witness. It seems clear that the idea of the 'Sonship' of Jesus has come to mean something fuller to us now than what it meant in John's own situation. In my previous chapter I explained the way in which a 'functional' understanding of the relationship of Jesus to the Word of God (ie a matter of *doing* and revealing exactly what God does and is) must end in an 'ontological' understanding (ie a matter of union of *being* with God). As the Spirit of God unveils the meaning and identity of Jesus within the meditation of the Church, there is a necessary and inevitable progression from one kind of understanding to the other. Just such a process is at work with the title 'Son of God', moving rightly from 'Son of God' to 'God the Son'. This truly unfolds who Jesus is. But we do need to remember that there is a journey of faith and thought which the early Christians were called to undertake, and we must be careful not to read back the fully achieved understanding into New Testament texts where this is not present.

The centrality of the person of Christ within our faith has meant that the question 'Who is Jesus Christ?' has naturally become an absolutely critical one for us. It is central to our faith that the identity of Jesus Christ be discovered and confessed. But when we ask, 'Who is Jesus Christ?' and the answer comes back quickly that 'Jesus is God!', we must be careful to give proper consideration to the delicate way that the New Testament expresses the relationship between Jesus the Son and God the Father.

It is in this connection that a fresh consideration of John's Gospel is vital since he has christology as one of his prime concerns. John employs a variety of titles and ideas to communicate his christology, the two most important being 'Son of God' and 'Word'. It is surely no accident that the translators of the New English Bible rendered John 1:1c as 'what God was, the Word was.' They were trying to reflect the fact that the precise relationship between Jesus the Son, or in this instance, the Word, and God the Father is a mysterious and delicate matter, something which strains the limits and tests the abilities of language to express adequately.

All of this is to suggest that we need to be clear in our minds what we mean when we come to describe Jesus as the 'Son of God'. Our understanding will be deepened if, in reading the New Testament, we do not assume that every declaration about his 'Son-ship' (his relationship to the Father), must be equated *in that context* with a declaration about his 'God-ship' (his place within the Trinity). Some of the most respected and influential bible students of our age have, with the best intentions, made or implied just such an equation. For instance, this seems to be the suggestion of John R.W. Stott when he says that Jesus's claims 'refer not just to his Messiahship but to his deity. His claim to be the Son of God was more than Messianic; it described the unique and eternal relationship with God which he possessed.'[2] In some ways this is perfectly natural and right given the traditions of our faith. But is it 'biblical', in the sense that it is a declaration explicitly made within the gospels?

The proper confession of the Church that 'Son of God = God the Son' can be employed in a way that reflects little of the rather tenuous and delicately poised manner in which such christological matters are expressed in the New Testament. Occasionally it is argued with a clearly polemical aim in mind, one which if not checked can violate not only the spirit of Christian tolerance and openness, but run right against the grain of the New Testament documents themselves. What does John's gospel have to say on this matter? Does the simple and final equation that 'Son of God' means 'God the Son' enable us to penetrate to the heart of John's christological teaching? Let us examine the idea of the 'Son of God' in John more closely and see if we can begin to make progress towards an answer to this question. Once we have done this we can then move on to explore how some models of christological growth can help us see the significance of 'Son of God' and 'Word' as used in John.

2. THE SON OF GOD AS 'THE SENT ONE'

The *Superman* films have enjoyed enormous popularity and have in their own way become a form of modern religious mythology. Given the slick Hollywood production and the stunning special effects, it is hardly surprising that they have become so successful. The films have at their heart quite an interesting parallel to the New Testament message, one focusing on Superman as being sent to Earth from 'outside' (in this case, the planet Krypton). It is interesting to note in *Superman* I the words said to the young infant (destined to become Superman) by his father Jor-El (Marlon Brando!) as he prepares to send him to Earth: 'All that I have I bequeath you, my son. You'll carry me inside you all the days of your life. You will see my life through yours, and yours through mine. The son becomes the father and the father the son.'

The parallels between a Johannine 'Son of God' christology and the films are quite striking.[3] For most people watching the film the underlying reliance upon the Johannine witness lies undetected, and it would probably be rejected by many devotees if it were pointed out or suggested. Yet the fact remains that strong parallels do exist, testifying no doubt to the enduring truth of the biblical witness and its power to appeal to the human spirit, even at an unconscious level. Let us explore the Johannine idea of the 'Son' more fully.

It is quite clear that John uses 'Son' language as one of his primary means of expressing his christological message about Jesus. Consider the following figures outlining John's use of terms:

'Son' (19 times) — 1:18; 3:16, 17, 35, 36 (twice); 5:19 (twice), 20, 21, 22, 23 (twice), 26; 6:40, 8:36; 14:13; 17:1 (twice).
'the Son of Man': (13 times) — 1:51; 3:13, 14; 5:27; 6:27, 53, 62; 8:28; 9:35; 12:23; 12:34 (twice); 13:31.
'the Son of God':(9 times) — 1:34, 49; 3:18; 5:25; 10:36; 11:4, 27; 19:7; 20:31.

Perhaps it should be mentioned that although 'Son of Man' and 'Son of God' arise from two quite different christological bases, they share a common theme, namely that of 'Son-ship'. It is in connection with this 'Son' imagery as a whole that the former title is briefly included in our discussions at this point. In some respects, the basic christological affirmation made by 'Son of Man' is quite distinct from that made through the title 'Son of God' or even 'Son'. While there is an aura of mystery surrounding the title 'Son of Man' as it appears in the Synoptics, in John the title serves mainly as a vehicle for the author's motif of 'descending and ascending' between heaven and earth. It might be described as essentially a spatially-based expression, concentrating on the relationship between heaven and earth and often using language involving 'lifting' from earth to heaven. This can be readily seen in 1:51 (the first appearance of the title) where Jesus declares to Nathanael that 'You will see the heavens opened and the angels ascending and descending on the Son of Man'. The same spatial imagery holds for many other 'Son of Man' passages, including 3:13–14, 6:62, 8:28 and 12:34. The title 'Son of God', on the other hand, serves mainly as a vehicle for the author's Father–Son motif; it might be described as essentially a relationally-based expression. Having said that, in some key passages it is extremely difficult to separate the three 'Son' titles into such distinct categories, since the overlap and interpenetration of ideas between the three christological titles is so great. John 5:25–7 is a classic case in point which contains all three titles in as many verses.

In addition to this statistical evidence about the use of 'Son' in John we also need to remember that 'Father' is by far the most common term for the idea of God in the Gospel (approximately 120 times depending on the textual variants adopted). Somewhat surprisingly, this is even more frequent a designation in John than the Greek term 'theos', which occurs about 76 times. On the basis of this statistical evidence Robin Scroggs writes that:

[John] wants to correlate as closely as possible Son and Father. Just as 'Father' is for him the most adequate designation of divine reality, so 'Son' is that which most appropriately discloses the meaning of Jesus Christ. Indeed, they must be understood together, virtually as one concept. And why? I would suggest that through this correlation John wants to point to the intimacy of the relation of Father and Son.[4]

Another interesting way of seeing the unity that exists in John's Gospel between Father and Son is by noting an additional feature — the fact that the Father is specifically said to *send* the Son in many of the key texts which discuss them together. Note this idea of 'sending', for example, in connection with the Greek verb 'apostellō' in 3:17, 34; 5:36, 38; 6:29, 57; 7:29; 8:42; 10:36; 11:42; 17:3, 8, 18, 21, 23, 25; 20:21; and in connection with the Greek verb 'pempō' in 4:34; 5:23, 24, 30, 37, 6:38, 39, 44; 7:16, 18, 28, 33; 8:16, 18, 26, 29; 9:4; 12:44, 45, 49; 13:16, 20; 14:24; 15:21; 16:5. Just in passing, it is important to note that this idea of 'sending' extends to the disciples as well. In no less than three instances Jesus relates his being sent by God to his own sending of the disciples (13:20; 17:18; 20:21).

It should be quite clear to us by now that the 'Father–Son' relationship is deeply imbedded within the Johannine message. But what was it originally meant to communicate? Granted that the 'Father sent the Son', how would that declaration have been understood by John's audience? What is the background to the idea of the 'Son of God' in John's time?

Here it is important to remember that within a Jewish context the idea of 'Son of God' was intimately connected with a burgeoning Messianism. In fact we could even say that 'Son of God' was a Messianic designation, a title of office to be brandished by the Messiah when he appeared in glory and thus linked with another Messianic title, 'Son of David'. Thus, in some Jewish quarters it was clearly a title associated with ideas of an eagerly-awaited, militaristic Messianic figure who would come to re-establish the Davidic kingship over the land of Israel. That is precisely how the idea of 'Son (of God)' is taken in the Psalms of Solomon, for instance, a Jewish document written at the time when the Roman armies of Pompey first came to capture Jerusalem in 48 BCE. Note Psalm of Solomon 17:21–22a: 'See, Lord, and raise up for them their king, the Son of David, to rule over your servant Israel in the time known to you, O God. Undergird him with the strength to destroy the unrighteous rulers, to purge Jerusalem from gentiles who trample her to destruction.'

This idea of a militaristic, 'Warrior' Messiah seems at first light a far cry from the Johannine 'Son of God/Messiah' link we are suggesting underlies the Gospel's christological message. Yet, we do have a number of other New Testament passages which adopt this 'Warrior' language as an image for the mission of Jesus and his followers. One only has to think about Revelation 19, for instance. The point to remember here is that John's 'Son of God' christology arises out of a creative milieu of Jewish Messianism; that is where it must be grounded, that is where its origins must be traced. This remains true even if we would want, in the very next breath, to insist rightly that in Jesus's own ministry, and indeed within the New Testament documents at large, the Messianic designation 'Son of God' is given new shape and direction. It is only when the Messianic background for 'Son of God' is taken seriously that the meaning of Jesus's baptism comes alive. In Mark 1:11 the heavenly declaration about the 'Son' is in fact a Messianic inauguration, a public act acknowledging Jesus as the accepted 'Son of God'.

So what does all of this mean? In the first instance it means that the Messianic basis for John's 'Son' christology has to be taken seriously. In John's own setting and within the minds of his audience (insofar as we can determine it) the 'Son-ship' of Jesus would have been understood in human, Messianic terms, not immediately divine ones. But in the second instance it means that we have somehow to account for the fact that the idea of Jesus as the 'Son of God' was not allowed to rest for very long on that human level. A 'higher' christological perspective was already developing and eventually won the day at Nicaea and Chalcedon. How do we describe the relationship between the later formulation of christology and the foundational New Testament documents, such as John, which contain those first experimental steps of explication? How do we explain the changes that have occurred in christological understanding? We turn now to consider some ways in which such christological change can perhaps be better understood.

3. MODELS OF CHRISTOLOGICAL CHANGE

No one should doubt that changes in christological understanding have occurred over the course of time. Any cursory examination of Church history will confirm this beyond reasonable doubt. Yet the reasons as to why and in which manner such changes might be explained are extremely complex, and the theological implications of them even more difficult to grasp. The question is thus not *whether*, but *why* changes occur.

C.F.D. Moule, in his stimulating book entitled *The Origin of Christology*, contrasts two models for understanding christological change: an 'evolutionary' model and a 'developmental' model. Moule himself opts for the second of these models, because he feels it is closer to the New Testament evidence and explains 'all the various estimates of Jesus reflected in the New Testament as, in essence, only attempts to describe what was already there from the beginning. They are not successive additions of something new, but only the drawing out and articulating of what is there.'[5] By contrast, the 'evolutionary' model suggests that changes might occur which are not simply inherent within the original christological declaration. Christological ideas would 'evolve' into new 'species', perhaps assimilating new ideas and meanings from different cultural settings, absorbing them as a new stage of christological expression comes forth, and resulting in fresh, creative understanding.

Fortunately we need not decide at this point whether one alone of the two models is correct. In point of fact both have something to commend them; each has its own strengths and weaknesses. The situation is very much like the one that exists in the realm of the physical sciences where different theoretical models are put forward by physicists to explain the phenomenon of light. Certain properties of light are best explained by a 'wave' model, while other properties are best explained by a 'particle' model. Yet, you cannot 'harmonize' the two theories; neither model is completely compatible with the other. In fact, both are needed to gain the fullest understanding of how light operates. The same holds true when we consider christology; some features of christological change are best understood through the 'evolutionary' model and others through the 'developmental' model. Both need to be used if we are to avail ourselves of every opportunity to understand the fullness of Johannine christology.

How does all of this work out in practice when we come to John's two central christological themes, namely his teaching about 'Son of God' and 'Logos'? At the risk of oversimplifying the point, I would like to suggest that in John's Gospel we have an opportunity to apply both models of christological change to the text and thereby come to a fuller comprehension of it. By this I mean to say that the Johannine idea of 'Son of God' is a prime example of a christological doctrine which follows the 'developmental ' model as it is taken up and shaped in the life of the Christian church in subsequent generations. At the same time the Johannine idea of the 'Logos' is a good example of a christological doctrine best understood as exemplifying, at least in John's *own* thought, the 'evolutionary' model. In my judgement, the subsequent christological developments concerning the 'Son of God' seen within the Nicene and Chalcedonian creeds are the unfolding of Johannine theology; they stand as its explication and there is a continuity of content. They demonstrate the direction in which Johannine theology was pointing through its declaration of Jesus as the 'Son of God', and are perfectly compatible with the witness of the Gospels.

On the other hand, we could say that with the doctrine of the 'Logos' John himself was not so much demonstrating an unfolding of an already established idea, but boldly striking out in a completely new direction, saying something never said before. John is attempting to say something so stunningly new and original that it becomes more appropriate to describe this christological shift by means of the 'evolutionary' model, as a sort of theological 'quantum leap'. No one would have expected that the declaration of the incarnation of the Word would be the 'natural' outcome of a wisdom theology. If unexpectedness is a hallmark of the 'evolutionary' model, then nowhere is it more accurately applied than here in John 1:1–14. Both models, the 'developmental' and the 'evolutionary' are useful in understanding the christological message of the Gospel of John.

Against this background of christological change, we can now see more clearly a truth which lies at the heart of the paradoxical nature of much of John's christological teaching.

4. THE SUBORDINATION OF THE SON

One of the most striking features of John's 'Son' christology is the fact that the Son is clearly presented as being subordinated to the Father. Nowhere is this more clear than in John 5 where again and again the dependence of the Son upon the Father is asserted. John 5:19 is a typical statement: 'Truly, truly, I say to you, the Son can do nothing of his own accord, but only what he sees the Father doing.' Other significant passages include 10:37–8 (where Jesus notes that he does the work assigned to him by the Father); 14:28 (where Jesus acknowledges that the Father is greater than he is); 17:4 (where Jesus glorifies the Father by accomplishing the work he has given him).

C.K. Barrett[6] comments on an essential point of such passages with these words: 'It is further to be observed that those notable Johannine passages that seem at first sight to proclaim most unambiguously the unity and equality of the Son with the Father are often set in contexts which if they do not deny at least qualify this theme, and place alongside it the theme of dependence, and indeed of subordination.' John is certainly not alone in this. A number of similar subordinational texts can be found within key passages of Pauline corpus, namely 1 Corinthians 15:28c and Philippians 2:11c.[7] But how widespread was this notion of 'subordination'? Has it been universally held within the Christian tradition?

It is perhaps worth quoting at this point the declaration about the 'Son' which is contained in the Nicene Creed of 325 CE. The creed affirms:

We believe... in one Lord Jesus Christ, the Son of God, begotten from the Father as only-begotten, that is, from the substance of the Father, God from God, light from light, true God from true God, begotten, not made, *homōousios* (of one substance) with the Father, through whom all things came into existence, the things in heaven and the things on the earth, who because of us men and our salvation came down and was incarnated, made man, suffered, and arose on the third day, ascended into heaven, comes to judge the living and the dead.[8]

The critical point that I would wish to call attention to is that there is no element of the subordination of the Son to the Father within the Nicene creed. There is nothing of this 'qualification' of which C.K. Barrett spoke. In spite of the fact that John's Gospel has served as the scriptural platform for much of the christological message contained within the creed, this essential Johannine feature is completely overlooked within the declaration. Why is this so?

The answer is surely that we see here a reflection of the struggle of the fourth century Church as the Arian controversy was being grappled with. To include the Johannine note of subordination of the Son to the Father would have seemed to concede a key theological point to the position of the Arian camp, who thought of 'the Son' as a supreme creature, but not fully divine. Both orthodox and heretic assumed that it was impossible for divine nature to include humility and subjection; that was better left explained as belonging to Jesus's *human* nature! After all, how could a view of God's nature which sees in him what the world calls power, might, and authority accommodate such a note of subordination? Rather than do this, the Nicene creed simply overlooks the Johannine note of subordination.

And yet the remarkable thing about John's Gospel is that it is able to hold together these two themes — Jesus's unity with God and his subordination to God. We could almost say that they exist in creative tension, each serving to define its counterpart. But what does that mean for us now? One of the important theological implications which arises out of this is that Jesus Christ, whom we would affirm as the incarnation of God, challenges us to consider afresh the very nature of God. Does our *theology* allow us seriously to consider a God whose very nature includes such self-depreciation? If we take the element of subordination contained within John seriously, we are left with no other credible option. In the end, we will find that our views of who God is must be stretched so as to include this note of humility. God is divine precisely in being humble, not despite it. Is that not what gives the incarnation its power and wonder, the fact that God stoops down to the level of humanity?

Finally, and most important for our ministries, this declaration of the subordination of Jesus Christ the Son to God the Father challenges us to think again about how we are to follow this model of subordination and humility in our relationships with each other, and, indeed, within the larger world. The New Testament again and again affirms that our ethical pattern in life is derivative; that is to say, it flows out of our relationship to Christ. We are to model ourselves on Jesus, to look to the resurrected Christ for our example and inspiration, as well as the source of our power for Christian living. As men and women called to be servants of God, the proclamation of this essential truth of the humility of God in Christ, which lies at the heart of our faith, remains one of our most difficult and demanding tasks. At the same time if it is done properly, if Christ-like humility is embodied faithfully by us, it can become our most satisfying joy in life.

We conclude our study of the Gospel of John with a prayer about the God who comes to us amidst the circumstances of life.[9] We do so remembering that it is in the coming of Jesus Christ to us that we see God revealed most clearly. I trust that through a careful study of the Gospel of John we can all be brought to a greater realization of Christ's presence with us, so that in and through him we encounter God afresh.

> Lord God, we adore you because you have come to us in the past:
> You have spoken to us in the Law of Israel.
> You have challenged us in the words of the prophets.
> You have shown us in Jesus what you are really like.
>
> Lord God, we adore you because you still come to us now:
> You come to us through other people and their love and concern for us.
> You come to us through men and women who need our help.
> You come to us as we worship with your people.
>
> Lord God, we adore you because you will come to us at the end:
> You will be with us at the hour of death.
> You will still reign supreme when all human institutions fail.
> You will still be God when our history has run its course.
> We welcome you, the God who comes.
> Come to us now in the power of Jesus Christ our Lord!

NOTES TO CHAPTER 9

1   Robin Scroggs, *Christology in Paul and John,* Proclamation Commentaries, (Fortress Press, Philadelphia, 1988), p. 63.

2   John Stott, *Basic Christianity,* (IVP, London, 1971), p. 26.

3   On these parallels, see the interesting article 'Chauvinist Messiah', by Ed Spivey, Jr., in *Sojourners,* March 1979. Robert Short, *The Gospel From Outer Space,* (Collins, Fount, London, 1983), pp. 40–4, also has a brief chapter on this. Commenting on Jor-El's speech in the film, Short says that: 'the script sounds as if it might have been ghost-written by the author of the Gospel of John.' (p. 40).

4   R. Scroggs, *Christology in Paul and John* (n.1 above) p. 69.

5   C.F.D. Moule, *The Origin of Christology* (Cambridge University Press, 1977), pp. 2-3.

6   C.K. Barrett, *Essays on John,* (ch.7 n.9 above) p. 23.

7   I have briefly discussed this matter within my *Jesus and God in Paul's Eschatology,* JSNT Supplement Series 19, (Sheffield Academic Press, 1987), pp. 158–163. It should not pass unnoticed that both 1 Corinthians 15:28c and Philippians 2:11c are taken by some scholars to be Pauline insertions into pre-Pauline hymns. Such a judgement is made largely on the assumption that the subordination clauses disrupt the form of the (reconstructed) hymns.

8   *The Trinitarian Controversy,* Sources of Early Christian Thought, edited by William G. Rusch, (Fortress Press, Philadelphia, 1980), p. 49.

9   Caryl Micklem, *Contemporary Prayers for Public Worship* (SCM Press, London, 1967). Reproduced by permission.

QUESTIONS FOR THOUGHT AND DISCUSSION

1.   Do you find C.F.D. Moule's distinction between a 'developmental model' and an 'evolutionary model' of christology helpful? What are the strengths and weaknesses of each model?

2.   Ernest Best, *From Text to Sermon* (ch.8 n.5 above) p. 115, comments: 'It is unlikely that many sermons will be preached directly on Christology yet those who preach are always drawing out the significance of Christ and need to be aware of the on-going discussion about Christology so that they present Jesus in such a way that he may be understood in a secular culture.' How might we best present Jesus in our modern secular culture?

3.   Examine closely the hymn books or chorus books you use regularly in worship. What sort of 'Son' image is presented within them? Do they retain the Johannine element of subordination and a sense of divine humility?

4.   Think back over your life and recall at least one person whom you think personified a Christ-like character. In what ways was this person an influence upon you? Was it because of something sacrificial that he or she did for you?

5.   Within a small-group setting ask each member to compose a list of words describing Jesus Christ. Have one person do this using only nouns, another using only adjectives, and another using only verbs. What does such an exercise tell us about the limitations of language in expressing christology? Make sure that you have a good English dictionary handy for the discussion afterwards.

X

An Annotated Bibliography on Commentaries

Within this chapter I would like to offer my comments about some of the many commentaries on John which are available. I have tried to include most of the English-language volumes of this century, including one or two that have been translated from German. Some of the best commentaries are now out of print and can be obtained only from used or second-hand sources.

I have tried to arrange my comments into several key areas, including price, availability, readability, and usefulness in preaching. With regard to availability, I have tried to give some indication about how easy it will be to obtain any given book. Within the areas of readability and usefulness in preaching, I have ranked the commentary on a 5-star basis. Thus:

*	=	Poor, not really worth considering, either boring or not relevant to the task at hand.
**	=	Fair, some worthwhile features, sometimes difficult to see how application can be made.
***	=	Standard, of mixed worth, predictable and tending towards reinforcement of what you already know.
****	=	Good, much that is of value, stimulating and interesting.
*****	=	Excellent, the best of its kind in this area, very challenging and worth having in your library.

The overall idea here is that the prospective buyer will have a rough guideline about how any given commentary fares in some of the key areas which will be of interest to a pastor or a leader in a congregation. I have also tried to give as much information as is possible about the bibliographical details of the various commentaries and have offered some additional comments, such as details about the author, which may be of interest to the reader.

The following list is arranged alphabetically according to the name of the author.

> Barrett, C.K., *The Gospel According to St. John,* 2nd Edition, (SPCK, London, 1978), 638 pages, £22.50 (First edition 1955)

Price Slightly expensive
Availability Still in print although it may have to be ordered. The first edition can

be found for about £10, but it is better to obtain the second edition if possible. The revision is extensive.

Readability *** Well written but does presume that the reader has a thorough grounding in Greek. The exegesis is exhaustive and yet stimulating, holding the attention well.

Usefulness in Preaching **** The strength of this commentary is its exegesis, but by the time you work through a section of text (the commentary is divided into 44 sections) you will be amazed at how well it prepares you for an expositional sermon. The 'Introduction' (covering nearly 150 pages!) is also an excellent way into such issues as date, theology of the gospel, intended audience.

Comments The author, now retired, was for many years Professor of Divinity at the University of Durham. He has an international reputation as a scholar of both the Johannine literature and the Pauline corpus. One special feature throughout is the attempt to explore John's knowledge of and reliance upon Mark in his Gospel.

> Beasley-Murray, George R., *John,* The Word Biblical Commentary 36, (Word Books, Waco, Texas, 1987), xcii + 441 pages, £18.95 (hardback) or about £8.95 (paperback).

Price Excellent value for money, particularly if you buy the (forthcoming) paperback edition.

Availability May have to be ordered from a bookshop.

Readability **** This is a very thorough one-volume commentary which is clearly written and beautifully laid out in stages (bibliography/translation/notes/setting/ comments). It is perhaps the most up-to-date volume available for listing secondary literature and contains a wealth of interaction with these works. Greek is needed to make the most of this commentary.

Usefulness in Preaching **** Very helpful discussion of most of the key theological themes in any given passage makes this a wonderful commentary to use in tackling the meaning of a text. The commentary is not specifically designed as a preacher's commentary but it does prepare one for the homiletical task admirably.

Comments The author is a prominent Baptist New Testament scholar whose international reputation has been established through a number of important exegetical writings. For many years he was Principal of Spurgeon's College, London. He remains one of the authoritative voices for a conservative-evangelical viewpoint.

> Bernard, John, *The Gospel According to St. John,* International Critical Commentary, 2 Volumes, (T & T Clark, Edinburgh, 1928), cxli + 740 pages, £14.95 per volume, (hardback).

Price Quite expensive for what it will contribute.

Availability Available new only at specialist bookshops or direct from the publisher. However, secondhand copies are sometimes found in obscure corners of village bookshops. Pay £5.00 at most for each secondhand volume; I do not advise buying it new.

Readability * This commentary is written primarily as a textual-critical guide to the gospel. It presumes a high degree of competence (and interest!) in Greek. Although occasionally some 'diamonds in the rough' will appear, this one will seem as dry as dust to most people.

Usefulness in Preaching * Minimal direct use for a preaching ministry. It is, however, an important place to go if you have a question about a textual variant or an obscure reading.

Comments The author died just shortly after completing the commentary in 1927. It is thus written before many of the higher-critical tools of modern scholarship were developed and it seems to lack a sense of application for our time. Volume 1 covers John 1:1–7:52 and Volume 2 covers 8:12–22:25 with 7:53–8:11 handled as an appendix.

> Brown, Raymond E., *The Gospel According to John,* 2 Volumes, The Anchor Bible, (Geoffrey Chapman, London, 1966 and 1970), cxlvi + 1208 pages, £27.50 per volume, (hardback).

Price Quite expensive but very good value for money.

Availability You probably will have to order this from a main-line bookshop although it has been in print for so long that you might be fortunate enough to find a secondhand copy.

Readability *** Quite a flowing style of writing but absolutely wearing at times. Brown is so thorough in his pursuit of an idea that at times you forget where it was that you were heading in the beginning. He uses his own translation and transliterates Greek throughout.

Usefulness in Preaching **** Perhaps one of the most useful commentaries that you can have within your library to assist you in preaching. This is because of the fact that Brown is so thorough that by the time you work through his treatment of a given passage you are very well-prepared to build a sermon. The abundance of excurses and appendices are also a bonus to this end. Every pastor should eventually aim to have a copy of this in his or her library.

Comments R.E. Brown is one of the most respected New Testament scholars of our day, and has a long association with Union Theological Seminary, New York City. Helpfully, this commentary attempts to identify five distinct stages in the composition of the Gospel. Occasionally Brown pursues a Roman Catholic agenda which may be a little distracting for some. Brown has also written the Anchor Bible volume on the Johannine epistles which carries through his ideas about the foundation and development of the Johannine community. Volume 1 covers John 1-12 and Volume 2 covers 13-22.

> Bruce, F.F., *The Gospel of John,* (Pickering & Inglis, Basingstoke, 1983), 425 pages, £8.95, (paperback).

Price Fairly good value for money.

Availability Many evangelical/Christian bookshops will stock this one. Readily available.

Readability * * * As is true with most of Bruce's writings, this commentary is very clear and easy to follow. Greek terms are transliterated to aid the non-specialist.

Usefulness in Preaching * * Bruce produces his own translation of the text (perhaps the single most important contribution of the commentary). I would describe this commentary as 'safe and conservative'; but is that what you really want from a commentary? I find that there is little to challenge me to think about the text in a fresh way here.

Comments Professor Bruce is now retired from a long and distinguished academic career at the University of Manchester. He is known internationally as a conservative biblical specialist and stands as perhaps the best modern scholar to have arisen from within the ranks of the Brethren tradition. A fairly extensive bibliography helps make the volume of some value to the inquisitive mind. A standard introduction (but alas, not very gripping!). An introduction of 27 pages is of some practical usefulness.

> Bultmann, Rudolf, *The Gospel of John,* translated by G.R. Beasley-Murray, (Basil Blackwell, Oxford, 1971), 744 pages, (hardback and paperback).

Price Excellent value for money, particularly if you are able to get a paperback copy. Secondhand paperback copies go for about £12.50, hardback copies for about £20.00.

Availability No longer in print, and difficult to obtain. The paperback edition can sometimes be found in second-hand bookshops.

Readability * * * Quite well written, but there are sections in which the amount of detail provided becomes a hindrance. In one or two sections the footnotes swamp the body of the commentary. Considering that this is a translation from a German commentary (which tend to be quite 'dense'), this is a remarkably entertaining volume to read.

Usefulness in Preaching * * * * There is a great deal that is of use here for preaching, providing that you are willing to struggle through the immense amount of material provided. The most important sections are on the relationship between humankind and God (such as the Lazarus episode of chapter 11).

Comments Written by one of the most influential New Testament interpreters of our age. Bultmann was for many years Professor of New Testament at Marburg, Germany (he died in 1976). This is perhaps the most stimulating commentary available on the gospel of John when it comes to insights into the human condition (Bultmann says that human being and its origins are intimately connected!). It is also very challenging in making us aware of how the gospel of grace meets us in the modern world. Bultmann's commentary is essentially a product of his form-critical mindset and is slightly out of date as a result. His redactional analyses of the text are a point of considerable scholarly debate and have been largely superseded now. Nevertheless, this should be read simply for the sheer joy of watching a man wrestle with the realities (as he sees them) of God's word. Read and enjoy this one!

> Fenton, John C., *St. John,* New Clarendon Bible (Oxford University Press, 1970), £5.50 (paperback).

Price A little expensive for what it offers. The price is high, no doubt, because it is part of the NCB series. You are paying for a name here! You should pay no more than £2.50 for a secondhand copy.

Availability Still in print. Readily available from most good bookshops. Many secondhand bookstores often have older editions. My advice is that you only buy a used copy of this one.

Readability *** Written in a very readable style, but unfortunately there is not a lot of substance to the commentary itself. It does reproduce the RSV text throughout, but this sometimes takes up half of any given page. The commentary does not require a working knowledge of Greek.

Usefulness in Preaching * This is definitely not designed as a commentary to aid you in your preaching. In fact it was originally aimed at helping students prepare for GCE 'A' levels.

Comments Written by a prominent Anglican, then teaching at St. Chad's College, Durham. Fenton is now a Canon of Christ Church, Oxford. Perhaps the best use that can be made of this commentary is within a small group Bible-study in which you might ask one of the members to lead discussion on a particular passage. Incidentally, the commentary does contain some very good black-and-white photographs of sites and ruins from the first-century world, one of the few to do so.

> Fenton, John, *Finding the Way through John,* (Mowbray, London, 1988), £5.95, 105 pages, (paperback).

Price A little bit expensive for a paperback.

Availability Readily available from many Christian bookshops.

Readability **** Highly enjoyable and easy to read. Written for the educated layman and/or lay minister. No Greek required.

Usefulness in Preaching ** The approach is to work through the Gospel section by section with approximately 4-5 pages of discussion being given to each chapter of the New Testament text. The book may profitably be used to help you begin thinking about the gospel passages as you prepare your sermons. A good first step, but you will need to progress to a more weighty commentary afterwards.

Comments John Fenton is Canon of Christ Church, Oxford and has written this book with an eye toward the popular market. It is designed to accompany a devotional study of the text. There are not a lot of new ideas or insights to challenge the informed student, but as providing a first go at the Gospel of John the book performs its task well.

Haenchen, Ernst, *A Commentary on the Gospel of John,* translated by Robert W. Funk, 2 Volumes, The Hermeneia Commentary Series, (Fortress Press, Philadelphia, 1984), xxx + 308 pages (Volume 1), xvii + 366 pages (Volume 2), £26.50 per volume, (hardback).

Price Expensive. Fair value for your money.
Availability Almost certainly will have to be ordered from a main-line bookshop.
Readability ** An interesting lay-out but, typical for a German author, very dense in its argumentation. Most will find this a real struggle. A high proficiency of Greek is essential.
Usefulness in Preaching ** This commentary series is perhaps the foremost on the frontier of historical-critical scholarship and thus will challenge the reader on all fronts. Unfortunately, this approach is not directly applicable to a preaching ministry and the usefulness of the commentary is severely limited on that score. Not a lot to help you here but you may want to turn to it if you are doing post-graduate work (if not, save your money!).
Comments The author taught New Testament at the University of Münster and was one of the leading German scholars of this century. The commentary was first published in German in 1980 following Haenchen's death and was compiled from his notes on the Gospel. He is not always the easiest of writers to follow (or agree with!), but his work remains a force to be reckoned with among specialists. The only other comment to be made about the commentary is that it conforms to the size and format of the rest of the Hermeneia series and therefore does not seem to fit on any normal bookshelf. Most irritating! Volume 1 covers John 1–6 and Volume 2, John 7–22.

Hendriksen, William, *The Gospel of John,* The New Testament Commentary, (Banner of Truth Trust, London, 1954), 507 pages, £11.95 (hardback).

Price Fair value for your money.
Availability Many conservative-evangelical Christian bookshops will stock it.
Readability ** Fairly well laid out with an accompanying outline to each section of the Gospel covered. Greek is useful to know but not essential. Several charts help to communicate the ideas being asserted.
Usefulness in Preaching ** To my mind this commentary is not very stimulating to read and skates over many of the most interesting theological issues of the Gospel. Instead, it argues an ultra-conservative line which at times seems blissfully ignorant of most of the historical-critical issues involved. The most positive contribution to preaching is the abundant textual cross-references (to both Old Testament and New Testament) and the references to the thoughts of the Reformers contained in the discussion.
Comments This volume is one of several by the author on the New Testament books. It is a series highly recommended by D.M. Lloyd-Jones and will no doubt appeal to

many on that basis alone. If you buy this, make sure that you do balance it with something which at least recognizes the interpretative issues of John (because this one unfortunately does not!).

> Hunter, A.M., *The Gospel According to John,* The Cambridge Bible Commentary, (Cambridge University Press, 1965), 205 pages, £8.50, (paperback), (Reprinted 1986).

Price Very expensive if it is bought for usefulness as a preaching tool.
Availability Many good bookshops will stock this. It is readily found in both hardback and paperback editions in secondhand stores. Look for a used copy for about £3.50.
Readability * * * Quite easy to follow and retaining something of Hunter's wonderful style in spite of the fact that he is not allowed to develop much within the remit of the CBC series. The text uses the NEB which is printed throughout and occupies a healthy percentage of each page. Greek proficiency is not required.
Usefulness in Preaching * * The problem here is simply that the commentary is not extensive enough. What is there is excellent and thoughtful and will be of value to the pastor, but it does need to be supplemented by a fuller-bodied work.
Comments A.M. Hunter will be known to many through his numerous writings on the New Testament. For many years he was Professor of Biblical Criticism at the University of Aberdeen. He has distinguished himself as one of the few scholars who is able to combine scholarly skill with a pastoral oversight. He succeeds as an excellent 'popularizer'.

> Lightfoot, R.H., *St. John's Gospel: A Commentary,* (Clarendon Press, Oxford, 1956), 368 pages, £11.95, (hardback), (Reprinted in 1983).

Price Good value for your money, especially if you are able to find a good secondhand copy.
Availability Recently back in print. Look for it in secondhand shops for about £8.00.
Readability * * * The approach of the commentary is to handle the Gospel text in three stages: text, exposition and notes. This is done so well that it makes the commentary a joy to read. It is tightly packed material but immensely enjoyable. Facility with Greek is not required although discussion of Greek terms is often made. Uses the RV of 1884 as its translation text.
Usefulness in Preaching * * * A surprising commentary in the sense that you will find yourself continually challenged and confronted with a fresh viewpoint. In this regard, the commentary is an excellent one for any pastor to have in his or her library.
Comments In my mind this is one of the most under-rated commentaries on John. Lightfoot was for many years a New Testament teacher at Oxford and was one of the most influential figures in introducing form criticism to these shores. He died in 1953. This commentary on John was almost completed when Lightfoot died and

the finishing touches have been made by C.F. Evans. One very interesting idea contained in the 'Introduction' is entitled 'The Portraiture of the Lord' and attempts to describe five different vantage points (the Multitude, the Jews, the Baptist, the Disciples, the World).

> Lindars, Barnabas, *The Gospel of John,* New Century Bible, (Marshall, Morgan & Scott, London, 1972), 648 pages, £10.50, (paperback), (Reprinted in 1987).

Price Good value for the money.
Availability Still in print. Readily available from many Christian bookshops.
Readability * * * Fairly readable style. The commentary is based upon the RSV text so knowledge of Greek is not a pre-requisite. The special phrases or words discussed are highlighted to make it an easy commentary to use.
Usefulness in Preaching * * * Primarily designed as an aid to fairly serious Bible-study. Certainly not a mine of illustrations, but contains some solid comments which can be worked into sermons. The exegesis is solid and judicious.
Comments The research for this volume was completed in 1969 so it is slightly dated. Still, it is a useful addition to a minister's library. The author is an Anglican Franciscan who teaches at the University of Manchester, and has distinguished himself as a scholar of both the Old Testament and the New Testament. The 'Introduction' (73 pages) is an added bonus in that it provides an excellent survey of most of the critical issues relating to the interpretation of John. The more I use this commentary the more I come to like it as a 'back-up' source.

> Magregor, G.H.C., *The Gospel of John,* Moffatt New Testament Commentary (Hodder & Stoughton, London, 1928), lxviii + 704 pages (hardback).

Price Fair value for your money.
Availability No longer in print. Secondhand copies are readily found for about £2.50 or £3.00. Don't pay more than that for it.
Readability * * Fairly readable style of presentation. This commentary reproduces the Moffatt translation. Knowledge of Greek is not essential, but the large number of textual cross-references may prove to be a bit distracting to some.
Usefulness in Preaching * * * Not a lot here to help you directly in your preaching ministry. Some good ideas are contained within the commentary but it is not sufficient in and of itself. You will need something more substantial to carry you through. A good second or third line of defence.
Comments G.H.C. Magregor wrote this while in the midst of a busy pastoral ministry in Glasgow and that does help make it of some value, despite the fact that it was written over 60 years ago. As with all commentaries dating from that long ago, there is an old-fashioned feel to it.

Marsh, John, *Saint John,* Pelican New Testament Commentary, (Penguin Books, Middlesex, 1968), 704 pages, £6.99 (paperback), (Reprinted 1979).

Price Good value for your money, particularly if you can find an older version of the paperback edition. Look for it in secondhand bookshops at about £3.00.
Availability Most bookshops will have it or be able to order it readily for you. This is the advantage of its being within the Penguin series.
Readability *** Easy to follow and quite flowing in its style. Some may find the smallness of print a problem. No knowledge of Greek is required. It is the sort of commentary that does not allow you to get bogged down in details and thereby miss the wood for the trees.
Usefulness in Preaching *** The purpose of this commentary is to strike a middle ground between academic scholarship and a devotional reading of the text. The commentary has succeeded in this task reasonably well and should be of help to the active pastor. You will need something more substantial to back it up, I am afraid.
Comments John Marsh was until his retirement Principal of Mansfield College, Oxford. Not a lot of interaction with other writers on John is provided here, which is something of a disappointment. There is a fairly helpful 'Introduction' (89 pages) which is succinct and contains a good outline of the Gospel as a whole.

Morris, Leon, *The Gospel According to John,* (The New International Commentary on the New Testament), (Eerdmans, Grand Rapids, Michigan, 1971), 936 pages, £23.50 (hardback), (Reprinted in 1979).

Price Quite expensive. Fair value for your money.
Availability May need to be ordered from a main-line bookshop, although some Christian bookshops may stock it. Watch out for older editions as they can be considerably cheaper than a new one.
Readability ** Not the most stimulating style of writing, I am afraid. It is all there, but so 'woodenly' presented that the commentary as a whole is disappointing.
Usefulness in Preaching *** I find myself with mixed feelings about this commentary. In itself it has little that is helpful in preparation for a sermon. However, it does contain quite a few cross-references to Old Testament texts, to the Reformers, etc., which are very helpful. I would describe it as 'solid' and conservative in its approach and argumentation.
Comments Leon Morris is known internationally as a conservative biblical scholar who taught for many years at Ridley College, Melbourne. This volume was first issued in Britain in the 'London Bible Commentary Series'. There are some helpful 'Notes' on key topics which will be of benefit.

Richardson, Alan, *Saint John,* Torch Bible Commentary, (SCM Press, London, 1959), 220 pages, £4.50 (paperback), (Reprinted in 1976).

Price Fair value for money.

Availability This is readily available in both hardback and paperback versions. You should be able to find a secondhand copy for less than £2.00 (do not pay more!). Be patient and wait for a used copy; they seem to be almost everywhere sooner or later.

Readability ** Quite easy to read but very lightweight in what it contains. The commentary is based primarily on the RV of 1884 and does not require any knowledge of Greek.

Usefulness in Preaching * Not a lot of value here for the working pastor. If you do not expect a lot from it, go ahead and buy it (you won't be disappointed that way!).

Comments Alan Richardson has here written a commentary which focuses on key phrases or terms as it progresses through the text. Once in a great while something of enduring value shows up. You may turn to it in a bible study and find its greatest usefulness there.

Sanders, J.N., (with B.A. Mastin), *The Gospel According to St. John,* Black's New Testament Commentaries, (A.&C. Black, London, 1968), 480 pages, £9.95 (paperback), (Reprinted in 1986).

Price Fair value for your money.

Availability Still in print after many years and readily found in older hardback version in some secondhand bookshops. You should be able to find a used copy for about £5.00. Buy one if you can find it at this price.

Readability ** Reads fairly well and is quite stimulating at times as it works through the text section by section. The commentary reproduces the RSV text and does use a fair amount of Greek. I do find that it can be a bit superficial at times.

Usefulness in Preaching ** A standard work which will cover most of the main issues with a fair degree of depth and sensitivity. The fact that it is a product of the late 60s does limit its usefulness as a direct help to preaching today. At times it does seem downright disappointing!

Comments This volume is a combined effort, with Mastin completing the work of Sanders who died prior to finishing the commentary. Nevertheless, the bulk of the commentary (namely, the discussion of chapters 1–15) is clearly the brainchild of Sanders, who was Dean of Peterhouse, Cambridge. The volume has a fairly comprehensive 'Introduction' section for its size which adequately covers matters of authorship, date, purposes, etc.

Schnackenburg, Rudolf, *The Gospel According to St. John,* translated by Kevin Smyth (Volume 1), Cecily Hastings, Francis McDonagh, David Smith, Richard Foley (Volume 2), David Smith and G.A. Kon (Volume 3), 3 volumes, (Burn & Oates, Tunbridge Wells, 1968, 1980, 1982), 638, 556, 510 pages, £30.00 per volume (hardback).

Price Very expensive, but excellent value for your money.
Availability Still in print although it probably will need to be ordered from a main-line bookshop.
Readability ***** Very well written and easy to follow. The commentary does demand a good knowledge of Greek in order to appreciate it fully. It is so exhaustive that at times it becomes almost too cumbersome to use, but it is a must for any serious study of John.
Usefulness in Preaching ***** The exegesis is not especially geared toward sermon preparation but it is a veritable gold mine of information about the text. The commentary does contain a total of 18 excurses on various key topics which may be put to good advantage when preparing a thematic sermon series. If you use this systematically to work through a section of John, you should have no trouble in producing a stimulating and challenging expository sermon.
Comments Perhaps the single most important work on John available today, this mammoth trilogy is by a renowned Roman Catholic scholar who teaches at the University of Würzburg. Schackenburg is such an honest exegete and strives for objectivity so stridently that you cannot help but admire him. Mortgage your house if you need to, but try to buy this set! You won't regret it. Volume 1 covers the Introductory matters and John 1–4, Volume 2 covers John 5–12 and Volume 3 covers 13–22.

Sloyan, Gerard, *John,* The Interpretation Commentary Series, (John Knox Press, Atlanta, 1988), 239 pages, £17.50.

Price A little bit expensive for what it has to offer.
Availability May have to be ordered through a main-line bookshop from the States.
Readability **** Very fluid style and easy to use. Greek is not essential in this commentary and this makes it a joy to read, especially for those who need a challenging commentary but are put off by the language requirement.
Usefulness in Preaching **** This commentary is specifically designed for teaching and preaching and should be carefully looked at by anyone wishing to buy a tool for homiletical use. The text is divided up into small sections suitable for a sermon or bible study with special attention being paid to the meaning of the passage. Some of the more technical exegetical details are overlooked as a result and you may need to use it in conjunction with another full-bodied commentary.
Comments The author is professor of Religion at Temple University in the United States and has produced a volume which has its eye on the needs of a working pastor. Although not written by a New Testament specialist the commentary does provide some valuable insights into how various passages have been interpreted in the history of the Christian Church.

Smith, D. Moody, *John,* The Proclamation Commentaries, (Fortress Press, Philadelphia, 1976), 114 pages, £7.50, (paperback).

Price A little expensive for a paperback, but well worth it!

Availability May have to be ordered from the UK distributor. Some large bookshops may have it in stock. Watch out for a forthcoming second edition. Secondhand copies may be found, if you are lucky, for about £4.00.

Readability **** An enjoyable book to read. The clarity and lucidity of the argumentation stand as a model of how to communicate deep theological ideas in readily understandable terms. Greek is not a prerequisite although transliteration of terms is to be found.

Usefulness in Preaching ***** This is not specifically designed to be a verse-by-verse commentary on the text of John. Rather, it is an interpretative commentary and the approach is to treat the theological themes of the Gospel. This means that it is ideal for the pastor and is a readily adaptable tool for an expository sermon series. It also has a full textual index at the back to help you find any discussion on a passage.

Comments D.M. Smith teaches New Testament at Duke University, North Carolina and is one of the leading Johannine scholars in the world today. He is extremely thorough and abreast with all of the latest research into his field, combining that expertise with a clear Christian commitment. Make sure that you have this in your library! You will turn to it again and again.

Tasker, R.V.G., *The Gospel According to St. John,* The Tyndale New Testament Commentaries, (IVP, Leicester, 1960), 237 pages, £4.25 (paperback).

Price Fairly good value for your money. Look for secondhand copies for about £2.00. Do not pay more for it!

Availability Readily available, but watch out! This volume is scheduled to be rewritten for the TNTC series. It might be better to wait for the new edition.

Readability *** Easy to follow and well laid-out. This is primarily designed as an introduction to laymen and teachers and thus it does have a bit of a 'popular' flavour to it. Knowledge of Greek is not needed. Built on the AV text.

Usefulness in Preaching ** This is perhaps one of the weakest volumes in the TNTC series and will not provide much that will stimulate the working pastor. One or two interesting ideas.

Comments Professor Tasker taught New Testament at King's College, London for many years. His own journey of faith was a remarkable pilgrimage to an increasingly evangelical perspective and some will find the commentary an interesting one from that viewpoint. However, it must be said that the commentary was written nearly 30 years ago and it reads as if a little old fashioned.

Temple, William, *Readings in St. John's Gospel,* First and Second Series, (Macmillan, London, 1945), £8.95, xxxiii + 412 pages, (hardback).

Price Recently back in print. Good value for money if you can find a secondhand combined volume (First and Second Series together).

Availability May have to be ordered from a main-line bookshop. Copies can usually be found in secondhand bookshops for about £3.00.

Readability ** Easy to read and well-written. I did find the fact that it is written in AV-like language a distraction. Uses the RV text of 1884 and requires no knowledge of Greek.

Usefulness in Preaching **** This book is not a commentary so much as a devotional study of John's Gospel. It does, however, work through the text systematically and can be used in conjunction with a good scholarly commentary. It contains a wealth of practical insights and pastoral ideas which have helped to make it something of a classic. Most will find it provides an excellent beginning for a sermon.

Comments William Temple was a very influential Archbishop of Canterbury of the last generation. Try and buy a copy of this if you can find it. Although it is dated, it will provide a useful balance to some of the more exegetical commentaries, containing some prayers and hymns which will be challenging. John is set out here as being a 'Five Act' work with a 'Prologue' and an 'Epilogue'.

Westcott, B.F., *The Gospel According to St. John,* (John Murray, London, 1900), xcvii + 307 pages (hardback).

Price You may be able to find a secondhand copy for about £5.00. I would not pay more than that for it.

Availability No longer in print, but watch for it in secondhand sources.

Readability *** A standard work which has proven itself over the years. This is one of the places where you can find a solid defence of the apostolic authorship of the Gospel including a full discussion of the relevant Apostolic Fathers. One big drawback for some is the fact that Greek (and Latin!) are essential to be able to appreciate the work. The AV text is given throughout.

Usefulness in Preaching *** Some real gems of insight are embedded within this commentary and it should not be neglected simply because it is the product of another generation.

Comments The author was for many years the Regius Professor of Divinity at Cambridge and completed the commentary in 1881. It is inevitably limited in its applicability as a result.

May I be so bold as to recommend the following three works as the best available purchases for a pastor's basic library on John?

    1   G.R. Beasley-Murray's volume as a single-volume commentary.

    2   D. Moody Smith's volume as a preaching aid.

    3   R. Schnackenburg's three-volume as a way to transform your whole approach to John's Gospel. I know it is expensive, but if you can somehow manage to buy this you will never regret it!